Praise for
Ireland's Saint

"Bury proves to be more than a mere dry historian; he turns out to be a fine storyteller as well, and his accounts of Patrick's spiritual duels with Druid priests for the heart and mind of the Irish king are quite gripping."   —History Book Club

"Editor-writer Sweeney gives Bury's 1905 biography of the legendary St. Patrick a greater contemporary context in this meticulously researched and presented work. . . . Bury wrote what Sweeney calls the 'ideal modern biography' of Patrick. . . . Sweeney assembles and rearranges material from Bury's original work and incorporates more of Patrick's own words, from his *Confession* and *Letter against Coroticus*. Sweeney's light edits to Bury's text clarify exactly what Patrick did in Ireland, noting that although he did convert some pagan kingdoms, he also was responsible for organizing Christians who were already there and connecting the island with the church of the Roman Empire."

—*Publishers Weekly*

Jon M. Sweeney is an independent scholar, culture critic, and book publisher. He is the editor and author of many books including *The Road to Assisi: The Essential Biography of St. Francis*, *The St. Francis Prayer Book*, and *The Pope Who Quit: A True Medieval Tale of Mystery, Death, and Salvation*, which was recently optioned by HBO, Inc. He lives with his wife and daughter in Evanston, Illinois.

J. B. Bury (1861–1927) was an Irish historian and an expert on the Greek and Roman Empires. He grew up in County Monaghan the son of an Anglican rector and was made a fellow of Trinity College in Dublin at the young age of 24. In 1902, Bury was appointed the prestigious Regius Professor of Modern History at Cambridge University, a position he held until his death. He wrote many scholarly works, including *History of the Later Roman Empire, Invasion of Europe by the Barbarians*, and this biography of St. Patrick of Ireland.

IRELAND'S SAINT

The Essential Biography of St. Patrick

Mosaic of St. Patrick, Westminster Cathedral, London

IRELAND'S SAINT

The Essential Biography of St. Patrick
BY J.B. BURY

EDITED WITH INTRODUCTION AND ANNOTATIONS BY
JON M. SWEENEY

PARACLETE PRESS
BREWSTER, MASSACHUSETTS

FOR
Sarah-Maria and Joseph,
who remind me of Patrick's words in the *Confession*,
"I ought to give thanks to God without ceasing."
—J.M.S.

2013 First and Second Printing This Format
2010 First Paperback Printing
2008 First Hardcover Printing

Ireland's Saint: The Essential Biography of St. Patrick

Copyright © 2008 by Jon M. Sweeney

ISBN: 978-1-61261-333-8

The Library of Congress has catalogued the hardcover edition as follows:
Bury, J. B. (John Bagnell), 1861–1927.
 Ireland's saint : the essential biography of St. Patrick / J.B. Bury ; introduction
and annotations by Jon M. Sweeney.—[New ed.].
  p. cm.
 Rev. ed.: The life of St. Patrick and his place in history, 1905.
 Includes index.
 ISBN-13: 978-1-55725-557-0
 1. Patrick, Saint, 373?–463? 2. Christian saints—Ireland—Biography. 3.
Ireland—Church history—To 1172. I. Bury, J. B. (John Bagnell), 1861–1927.
Life of St. Patrick and his place in history. II. Title.

 BX4700.P3B8 2008

 270.2092—dc22   2008017071

10 9 8 7 6 5 4 3 2

Published by Paraclete Press
Brewster, Massachusetts
www.paracletepress.com
Printed in the United States of America

CONTENTS

INTRODUCTION

First published in 1905, John Bagnell Bury's (1861–1927) biography of St. Patrick of Ireland was the most influential study of the saint ever written up until that point. Bury's scholarship and conclusions directed the understanding of Patrick for at least a half century. Almost immediately, for instance, he overturned long-standing tradition that held that Patrick's mission lasted sixty years and the saint died in 493. Bury said Patrick's mission was only thirty years, the additional thirty were added by early hagiographers, and Patrick passed away in 461.

The original title of Bury's book was *The Life of St. Patrick and His Place in History*. Bury was an Irish historian, and an expert on the Greek and Roman Empires. He was also a Protestant, which might be unnecessary to mention under other circumstances; however, in the case of Irish history, it is unavoidable. He grew up in County Monaghan, the son of an Anglican rector. He was made a fellow of Trinity College in Dublin at the young age of twenty-four, and became recognized as expert in ancient, medieval, and modern history over the course of the next decades. In 1902, Bury was appointed the prestigious Regius Professor of Modern History at Cambridge University, a position he held until his death. *Modern*, in this instance, refers to all but ancient. Subsequent holders of the title have included George Macaulay Trevelyan, Herbert Butterfield, and William Owen Chadwick. A senior professorship by the same name exists at Oxford.

As he mentions in the first sentence of his original preface, Bury was attracted to the subject of St. Patrick "not as an important crisis in the history of Ireland, but, in the first place, as an appendix to the history of the Roman Empire, illustrating the emanations of its influence beyond its own frontiers." Bury's earlier writings spanned the ancient Greeks and Romans, throughout the Middle Ages, and into Victorian history. But he was considered expert, most of all, on the later Roman Empire. Some of his many writings on the subject include *History of the Later Roman Empire* (still in print in 2 volumes), *Invasion of Europe by the Barbarians* (recently reissued), and *History of the Eastern Roman Empire*. One of the primary emphases of his biography of Patrick is to place the Ireland of Patrick's day in the proper historical context, as influenced by the Germanic and Scandinavian invasions of the third to ninth centuries, but also, in many ways, to portray it as stubbornly apart from the empire. His biography of Patrick has been accurately described as "a postscript to the author's history of the later Roman Empire, dealing with the final episode in the spread of Roman civilization (which by this time happened to include Christianity also) among the barbarian peoples" (Binchy, 10).

Many scholars today argue with Bury's conclusions, saying that we cannot know as much as he claims to have discovered in the sources. "[The] Patrick of current mythology has been put together . . . mainly from an oblique inheritance from a long series of Lives," writes one of these (Thomas, 309). In other words, Bury may have brought Patrick scholarship into the modern era, but he still contributes to the perpetuation of stories we cannot fully substantiate. According to this line of thinking, only the writings of Patrick—the *Confession*, written when Patrick was an old man responding to charges made against him by British priests, and the *Letter Against Coroticus*, written somewhat earlier—are reliable witnesses to the facts of

Patrick's life and work. This is all that such scholars say that we can know for certain about Patrick's life:

- He was an old man when he wrote his *Confession*, and his Latin was unskilled.
- Patrick's father was named Calpurnius. He was a deacon.
- Patrick's grandfather was named Potitus, and a presbyter in his village in Britain.
- At 16, Patrick was kidnapped by pirates and taken to Ireland.
- His faith was kindled while in captivity in Ireland.
- He worked as a shepherd while in captivity, and he heard the "voice" of God speak to him.
- After six years, he fled Ireland stowed away on a ship. The ship traveled for three days until reaching land.
- After a harsh time with no food, Patrick and his companions found a herd of pigs and also ate honey from discovered hives.
- Patrick visited his parents in Britain a few years after he escaped from Ireland.
- He claimed to have baptized thousands of people while in Ireland.

Bury would agree with all of these items, but he also fills in additional details and challenges many others from legend and tradition and other medieval texts, creating a portrait that tells us far more than these simple "facts," and yet, stops far short of hagiography. His is the ideal modern biography.

Bury was one of the leaders among historians at the turn of the twentieth century who desired to transform scholarship and modern understanding of the past using critical tools of analysis. In this way, he was in solidarity with two generations of contemporaries, such as the great Ernest Renan (d. 1892), author of *Life of Jesus*, and Paul Sabatier (d. 1928), author of the influential biography of Francis of Assisi recently republished as *The Road to Assisi*. In one of Bury's most influential works, *A History of Freedom of Thought* (1913), he articulates how superstition, custom, and intellectual laziness have always hindered the progress of knowledge:

> If the social structure, including the whole body of customs and opinions, is associated intimately with religious belief and is supposed to be under divine patronage, criticism of the social order savors of impiety, while criticism of the religious belief is a direct challenge to the wrath of supernatural powers.
>
> The psychological motives which produce a conservative spirit hostile to new ideas are reinforced by the active opposition of certain powerful sections of the community, such as a class, a caste, or a priesthood, whose interests are bound up with the maintenance of the established order and the ideas on which it rests.
>
> Let us suppose, for instance, that people believe solar eclipses are signs employed by their Deity for the special purpose of communicating useful information to them, and that a clever man discovers the true cause of eclipses. His compatriots in the first place dislike his discovery because they find it very difficult to reconcile with their other ideas; in the second place, it disturbs them, because it upsets an arrangement which they consider highly advantageous to their community; finally, it frightens them, as an offense to their Divinity. The priests, one of whose functions is to interpret the divine signs, are alarmed and enraged at a doctrine which menaces their power.

In prehistoric days, these motives, operating strongly, must have made change slow in communities which progressed, and hindered some communities from progressing at all. But they have continued to operate more or less throughout history, obstructing knowledge and progress. (Bury, 9–11)

Bury is a clear and precise writer. But he is also one for metaphor and the delicate turn of phrase. At times, such as this one from chapter 3, he sounds almost like a poet: "But as Patrick grew up, the waves were already gathering, to close slowly over the island, and to sweep the whole of western Europe." We see in the same chapter a good example of Bury's ability to tell a story; he chronicles the invasions of the Picts, Scots, and Saxons upon the British isle in the fourth century, foreshadowing what must have been felt by Patrick's father, Calpurnius, when he "shared in the agonies that Britain felt in those two terrible years when she was attacked on all sides by Pict, by Scot, and by Saxon, when Theodosius, the great Emperor's father, had to come in haste and use all his strength to deliver the province from the barbarians. In the valley of the Severn the foes whom the Britons dreaded were Irish freebooters, and surely in those years their pirate crafts sailed up the river and brought death and ruin to many."

Still, as one Irish historian has put it, "this sturdy Rationalist [meaning, Bury] shows a curious tenderness towards the legendary material as a whole" (Binchy, 10). In other words, this biography is critical, but also sympathetic to the tradition and legends surrounding the saint.

A more recent biographer of Patrick has written, "Bury was possibly the most learned historian produced by the British Isles in the twentieth century. He knew all the European languages except three; and his familiarity with the scholarly literature of Europe was unmatched. . . . The result was such a work of scholarship as seemed to be the last word on Patrick" (Thompson, 176). But, of course, it wasn't, and subsequent researchers have found much to add and amend in Bury's famous account.

Additions and Changes to This Edition

Most contested among Bury's assumptions is the idea that the seventh-century biography of Patrick written by Muirchu is to be trusted. As mentioned above, recent historians often argue that the only truly reliable sources for knowing Patrick's life and beliefs come from the saint's own writings. For this reason, the present edition of Bury's important book includes many sidebar notes that add the thoughts (and occasional corrections) of more recent historians on various issues. Also, in the spirit of Bury's account, several sidebars provide portions of Patrick's own writings that have a bearing on the points being made. I have also plumbed the wealth of novels, poems, legends, art, theology, and other writings that serve to fill in the picture of Patrick drawn in Bury's account.

Other changes have been made to the original edition in creating the present one. For example, I have taken what was originally Bury's excellent summary chapter, "Patrick's Place in History," and made it his first. The style of biographical writing a century ago was different than it is today. It used to be that the biographer would tell his tale from beginning to end, only to unleash his most detailed opinions in a concluding chapter, followed by a voluminous amount of additional material, including refutations of other scholars, discursive analyses of key points, and so on, in various appendices. I have tried to cull the best of this latter material from the original edition and disperse it throughout where it properly belongs today, speaking straightforwardly to the reader. Many sentences and paragraphs that originally appeared in the notes and appendices sections of Bury's biography have been incorporated into the main body of the biography.

I have updated the language of Bury's prose, altering the style and sentence structure only when necessary to suit a more contemporary reader. Bury's ubiquitous double negatives have been altered whenever it seemed reasonable to do so. In some cases, I have used more recent, agreed-upon spellings, such as Pechenegs instead of Patzinaks for the nomadic people of the Asian steppes once converted by St. Bruno of Querfurt. Throughout the work, I have added dates after the names of important figures and made other invisible additions aimed at an appreciation of the biography for today. I have tried to provide the source of quotations made by Bury without attribution because he was writing for an audience that had a much larger religious literacy than we do today; a few of these are quotations from the Bible, and in these cases, I have changed the renderings to the New Revised Standard Version translation. I have also quietly changed a very few mistakes that Bury made, in the judgment of later scholars. For instance, in the chapter on Patrick's sojourn in Gaul after his escape from slavery in Ireland, Bury tells of his staying at the monastery of Lerinus. The Lerins islands, off the coast of France at Cannes, were made famous in the fourth century by St. Eucherius of Lyon, who was married before he became a hermit on the neighboring island of Lero. Bury mentions Eucherius's wife, Galla, but probably makes the mistake of assigning her to living together with her husband in hermit life. Later scholars seem to universally agree that it was only after his wife's death that Eucherius became a hermit.

I also have no doubt that today's reader wants to read more of Patrick's two writings—the *Confession* and the *Letter Against Coroticus*—in his own words. I have incorporated some of these into the book; they are taken from the translation given in the classic work published in New York in 1880, *The Most Ancient Lives of Saint Patrick, Including the Life by Jocelin, Hitherto Unpublished in America, and His Extant Writings*, by Rev. James O'Leary, D.D., fifth edition, modified only slightly. I have also included a prose translation of the bulk of the "Hymn of St. Seachnaill," in chapter 10.

Bury's Balanced Perspective

In his original preface, Bury wrote, "When I came to Patrick, I found it impossible to gain any clear conception of the man and his work. The subject was wrapped in obscurity, and this obscurity was encircled by an atmosphere of controversy and conjecture. Doubt of the very existence of St. Patrick had been entertained. . . . It was at once evident that the material had never been critically sifted, and that it would be necessary to begin at the beginning, almost as if nothing had been done, in a field where much had been written."

He went on to explain that the present biography was necessary because of the way the author methodically examined the original sources—perhaps for the first time by a modern scholar. Bury described his attempt to be impartial by referring to himself as "one whose interest in the subject is purely intellectual." Such a comment says more about his era than about the man. It is impossible to read this biography without feeling the passionate interest that the author had for his subject. And the fact that the author was a Protestant is perhaps what led him to also write in his original preface, "I will not anticipate my conclusions here, but I may say that they tend to show that the Roman Catholic conception of St. Patrick's work is, generally, nearer to historical fact than the views of some anti-Catholic clergy." All in all, this is a portrait for the ages.

As a modern historian writing at the beginning of modern religious history writing, Bury makes very few comments about Patrick's direct influence on the spiritual life of the Irish, or anyone else. Bury was quite modern in this respect, trying to keep fact apart from feeling, and the spiritual away from the ecclesiastical, in his accounts. My concerns are somewhat different, and I have added some sidebars with reflections on the spiritual import of Patrick throughout the work.

"Patrick's mission to the Irish had only been a limited success when he died, and since his greatness was not appreciated by the generation or two which followed—they did not even remember where his body was buried—it is not surprising that there are no early representations of him." (Thompson, 160)

Why does the study of St. Patrick matter today? If you have come to this book with questions and curiosity of your own, I hope you will find much to engage you here. One of the best summaries of Patrick's spirituality that I have encountered is this: "One of our most ancient manuscripts, the *Book of Armagh*, tells us that Patrick wished the Irish to have two phrases ever on their lips, *Kyrie Eleison* and *Deo Gratias*; Lord have mercy, and Thanks be to God. It was between these two prayers that Patrick lived out his own full and saintly life. It is where we, too, will find the fullness of life—trusting in the forgiveness of the One who loves us, and eternally grateful for everything" (O Riordain, 20).

IRELAND'S
SAINT

The Essential Biography of St. Patrick

CHAPTER ONE

Patrick's Place in History

There are two extreme and opposite views about the scope and dimensions of St. Patrick's work in Ireland. The older view is that he introduced the Christian religion and converted the whole island. The more recent view holds that the sphere of his activity was restricted to the one, small province of Leinster on the eastern seaboard. This second opinion is refuted by a critical examination of the sources and by its own incapacity to explain the facts. The first view, meanwhile, cannot be sustained either because clear evidence exists that there were Christian communities in Ireland before Patrick arrived.

Foundations had been laid for the faith sporadically here and there before Patrick ever arrived. This does not, however, deprive him of his eminent significance. Patrick did three things. He organized the Christianity which already existed. He converted kingdoms which were still pagan, especially in the west. And he brought Ireland into connection with

More about Leinster

Leinster has probably always been the most populated of the four provinces of Ireland (Connaught, Leinster, Munster, Ulster). It is the closest in proximity—just across the Irish Sea—from England. Dublin, the capital of the Republic of Ireland, is located in Leinster, as is Maynooth, the location of the national seminary. Leinster House is the seat of the National Parliament of Ireland. St. Brigid of Ireland was also from Leinster. Her mother was a Pictish slave who was baptized by St. Patrick, and her father was at one time the pagan Scottish king of the province.

the church of the empire, making Ireland formally part of universal Christendom.

These three aspects of his work will be illustrated in the following pages. Patrick's achievements as organizer of a church and as propagator of his faith made Christianity a living force in Ireland never to be extinguished. Before him, it might have been in danger of extinction through predominant paganism. After him, it became the religion of Ireland, though paganism did not completely disappear. He did not introduce Christianity so much as he secured its permanence, shaped its course, and made it a power in the land.

Pytheas—the First Explorer of the Isle of Ireland

Pytheas was the first explorer from the continent of Europe to see Ireland. Sometime between 330 and 300 BC, the merchant-explorer left his home city of Marseilles, made his way around Spain, and set out westward. In those ancient days, the lands of Britain, Ireland, and Scotland were the undiscovered north and west. Pytheas circumnavigated the entire island of Britain. "This enabled him to report, correctly enough, that the island was shaped like a triangle. . . . He established the location of Britain ('it extends obliquely along Europe') and probably of Ireland, and made several visits into the interior of the former to observe the inhabitants" (Casson, 138).

No less significant, though more easily overlooked, Patrick played a role in bringing Ireland into a new connection with Rome and the empire. Ordinary communication, as we will see, had been maintained for ages with Britain, Gaul, and Spain; but now the island was brought into a more direct and intimate association with western Europe by becoming an organized part of the Christian world. There had been constant contact before, but this was the first link.

The historical importance of this new bond, which marks an epoch in the history of

22

Ireland as a European country, was somewhat obscured through circumstances after Patrick's death. At that time, the Irish Church did not sever the link he had forged, and did not dream of repudiating its incorporation as a part of Christendom, but they did go ways of their own, developing along eccentric lines. Relations with the center were suspended, and this suspension seems to have been due to two causes.

An instinct of tribal independence, combined with the powerful attraction the Irish found in monasticism, promoted individualism and disorganization. Monastic institutions tended to override the Episcopal organization founded by Patrick, and the resulting disunity wasn't favorable to maintaining a practical solidarity with the rest of Christendom. But it was not entirely due to the self-will and self-confidence of the Irish that they drifted from his moorings. Political changes on the continent must have also had their effect on the situation. If it were not for the decline of imperial power and the dismemberment of the empire in western Europe, the isolation and eccentricity of the Irish Church in the sixth century would not have been so remarkable. The bishops of Rome—from Leo I (440–461) to Gregory the Great (590–604)—were in no position to concern themselves with the drift of ecclesiastical affairs in the islands of the north. No sooner had Pope Gregory accomplished his great revival and augmentation of the authority of the Roman see in the west than the movement began which gradually brought Ireland back within the confederation. The renewal of the union with continental Christianity in the seventh century was simply a return by the church in Ireland to the system established by Patrick and his coadjutors. I wouldn't be surprised if, during that period of revival, people looked back with a more intense interest to Patrick's work and exalted his memory more than ever.

Tendencies that asserted themselves after Patrick's death were part of a general relapse. People returned to some practices that had been adopted in the Christian communities that existed before his arrival on the scene. An old practice of dating the Easter celebration, which Patrick had attempted to replace, was, for instance, resumed. Perhaps too, the Druid tonsure from ear to ear, which had been used by earlier Irish Christians, prevailed after Patrick's death.

Birth and Death in the Ancient World

Why do we often know the death dates (the specific month and day) for ancient and medieval figures with certainty, but often seem to estimate their birth years? In earlier centuries, the birth of a child was not the celebration and occasion that it is today. Many children were born to a family, and many also died in childbirth. Those people that went on to do important and public things were honored in their lifetimes, and remembered in their deaths. Also, death often meant martyrdom for people such as missionaries, and martyrdom usually led to sainthood. Saints have always been remembered in Catholic and other churches on the exact day of their death, or new life.

Compared to Other Missionaries of His Time

Patrick's work may be illustrated by comparing him with other bearers of the Christian message to the people of northern and central Europe. These are his contemporaries and near-contemporaries.

There were those who traveled among people that were entirely heathen, such as the Saxon St. Willibrord (ca. 658–739) to the Frisians in what is now The Netherlands; Adalbert of Prague (ca. 956–997) to the Hungarians and Prussians; or St. Bruno of Querfurt (ca. 970–1009) to the nomadic Pechenegs among the steppes of the Ural Mountains. Patrick's mission also bears some resemblance to those of St. Columba (521–597) in Caledonia. Columba went to organize and maintain Christianity among the Irish Dalriadan settlers and to convert the neighboring Pictish heathen, just as Patrick went to organize as well as to propagate his faith. But while these conditions of their tasks were similar, their works were quite different. It was Patrick's aim to draw Ireland into close intimacy with continental Christianity, while Columba represented in Ireland tendencies opposed to the Patrician tradition. Columba had no aims to intimacy with Rome, and he established in north Britain a church which offered a strenuous resistance to unity.

Dalriadans. One of the tribal clans that dominated northern Ireland in the ancient era, eventually expanding to include the islands of western Scotland.

Picts. Tribes of central and northern Scotland. Various tribes were ruled by separate kings who lived in various degrees of cooperation. The name "Pict" appears to derive from the Latin noun *Picti* meaning "tattooed" or "pictured" people. St. Patrick wrote of the "apostate Picts" who were in need of conversion from their various forms of heathenism and polytheism. Pictland is now known as the Isle of Iona.

St. Columba traveled to Scotland for the first time in 563, at least sixty-five years after the death of Patrick.

The closest likeness to Patrick is more likely St. Boniface (ca. 672–754), the Saxon. Like Patrick and Columba, Boniface set out to further the faith in regions where it was minimally known, and introduce it into regions where it had never penetrated. But, like Patrick and unlike Columba, he was in touch with the rest of western Christendom.

The political and geographical circumstances were different for Boniface. He was backed by the Frankish Empire; he was

The Franks, Wulfilas, and Two Saints

The Frankish Empire was not so much an empire as it was a loose confederation of barbarian tribes living along the northern borders of the Rhine River, in what is today France, Belgium, and parts of The Netherlands. They were Germanic people. Toward the end of the fifth century, two centuries before Boniface, the Frankish king Clovis converted to Christianity, bringing the Franks ever closer to what was left of the Roman Empire at that time.

Wulfilas is credited, as Bury says, with originating Gothic literature by his translation of the Bible into Gothic. Sts. Cyril and Methodius were Greek brothers and missionaries. Experts at Aramaic, Hebrew, and other languages, they are also credited with originating an alphabet—the Glagolitic—used in Slavonic manuscripts before the creation of Cyrillic.

nearer Rome and in frequent communication with the popes, and the popes of that day had an authority far greater than the popes before Gregory the Great. If Patrick looked with reverence to Rome as the apostolic seat, Boniface looked to Rome far more intently. In Patrick's day, the Roman Empire meant a great deal more than the Roman see; in the days of Boniface, the pope was still a subject of the emperor, but the emperor was far away in Constantinople; to a bishop in Gaul or Britain it was the bishop of Old Rome who, apart from the authority of his see, seemed to represent the traditions of Roman Christendom. But for both of them—Patrick and Boniface—their work was to draw new lands within the boundaries of Christian unity, which was closely identified at that time with the Roman name.

St. Patrick did not do for the Scots what Wulfilas (ca. 311–ca. 381) did for the Goths, or Cyril and Methodius (ninth century) did for the Slavs. He did not translate the sacred books of his religion into Irish or found a national religious literature. The fame of Wulfilas and Cyril rests entirely upon their literary achievements, not on their success at converting barbarians. The Gothic Bible of Wulfilas was available for the Vandals and other Germans whose speech was close to Gothic. The importance of the Slavonic apostles, Cyril and his brother Methodius, is due to the fact that the literature they initiated was available for Bulgarians and Russians.

What Patrick did was diffuse a knowledge of Latin in Ireland. We know that this is what he did, rather than create a national ecclesiastical language, because of the rise of the schools of learning which distinguished Ireland in the sixth and seventh centuries. From a national point of view the policy may be criticized; but from a theological perspective the advantage was clear: these Latin schools opened the native clergy to the whole body of patristic literature and saved the Irish the trouble of translation and the chances of error that may creep in.

This represents a sizeable difference between eastern and western Christianity in Patrick's era. During the reign of the Eastern Emperor Theodosius II (408–450) there was a Syrian as well as a Greek ecclesiastical literature. In Armenia there was an Armenian; in Egypt there was Coptic. But in the realm of Theodosius II's cousin and colleague, Valentinian III (423–455), there was only one ecclesiastical language, the speech of Rome itself. The reason was that Latin had become the universal language in the western provinces, which conditioned the whole growth of western Christendom. In the east, where this unity of tongue did not exist, no policy was adopted for imposing Greek on any new people that might be brought into connection with the church of Constantinople. In the west, the community formed by the Latin tongue powerfully conduced to the realization of the *unitas ecclesiae*. The case of Ireland shows how potent this influence was.

Christianity in the Outer Empire

"By the end of Constantine's reign, in 337, Christianity was well on its way to becoming the dominant religion in the eastern part of the Roman world. But in the less populous and more agrarian West, evangelism proceeded much more slowly." (Freeman, 57)

If Patrick had called a sacred literature into being for the Scots, such as Cyril initiated for the Slavs, we may be sure that the independent tendencies in the Irish faithful, which were already strongly marked in the sixth century, would have been more permanent in promoting isolation and aloofness. The successful movement of the following century that drew Ireland back into outward harmony and more active communion with the Western Church would have been more difficult and may possibly have failed. If Gaelic had been established by Patrick as the ecclesiastical tongue of Ireland, the reformers who in the seventh century sought to abolish idiosyncrasies and restore uniformity might have caused a rupture in the Irish Church which would have needed many years to heal. The Latin language was one of the *arcane imperii*, or "state secrets," of the Catholic Church.

It is true that the Irish Church progressed along certain lines that Patrick didn't contemplate and wouldn't have approved. But it would be untrue to say that his work was undone after his death. The schools of learning, for which the Scots became famous a few generations later, stood in contrast to Patrick's own illiterateness. But they owed their rise to the contact with Roman ideas and the acquaintance with Roman literature which his labors, more than anything else, lifted within the horizon of Ireland. It was not only the religion but also the language attached to it that inaugurated a new period of culture for the island and opened a wider outlook on the universe. The Irish were soon busily engaged in trying to work their own past into the fabric of ecumenical history, to synchronize their insular memories with the annals of Rome and Greece, and find a nook for their remote land in the story of the world.

All of these considerations may help to bring into focus the place that Patrick holds in the history of Europe. Judged by what he actually compassed, he must be placed along with the most efficient of those who took part in spreading the Christian faith beyond the boundaries of the Roman Empire. He was endowed with abundant enthusiasm, and stands in quite a different rank from the apostle of England, in whom this same enthusiasm was lacking: Augustine of Canterbury (d. 604), the messenger and instrument of Pope Gregory the Great.

Patrick was no mere messenger or instrument. He had a strong personality and great initiative. He depended on himself, or, as he would have said, on divine guidance. He was not in constant communication with Popes Sixtus III or Leo I, or any superior. He was thrown upon the resources of his own judgment. Yet no less than Augustine, no less than Boniface, he was the bearer of the Roman idea.

The pope had not yet become a spiritual Caesar Augustus, as he is at the present day. In the universal order, he was still to be overshadowed for generations by the emperor. The Roman idea at this stage didn't mean the idea of subjection to the Roman see, but of Christianity as the religion of the Roman Empire. It was as impossible for Patrick as it was impossible for the high-king of Ireland to divorce the idea of the church from the idea of the empire. Christianity was marked off from all other religions as the religion of the Romans in the wider political sense of the imperial name. If Christianity aspired to be ecumenical in theory, Rome had aspired in theory to realize universal sway before Christianity appeared.

It was Patrick with his auxiliaries who bore to the shores of Ireland the vessel of Rome's influence, along with the sacred mysteries of Rome's faith. He brought a new land into the spiritual federation which was so closely bound up with Rome—*nexuque pio longinqua reuinxit.*

Latin Quotes

J.B. Bury wrote in an era when most children in England and America learned Latin in school. He often quoted Latin phrases without providing English translations. This concluding quote is from the ancient Roman poet Claudian, writing with affection about the heroic past of the Roman Empire. The complete line is *Quos domuit nexuque pio longinqua reuinxit,* "She bound together the most remote regions, with a tie of loyalty." As one of Bury's contemporaries pointed out, "The Syrian, the Pannonian, the Briton, the Spaniard, still called himself a Roman. . . . St. Patrick (a younger contemporary of Claudian), in his Epistle to Coroticus, speaks of the Christians of Gaul as Romans" (Bryce, 9). The unity of the ancient and universal church, and Patrick's role in securing that unity for the Irish, is the primary theme of Bury's biography.

CHAPTER TWO
The Spread of Christianity
beyond the Roman Empire

The movements and wanderings, settlements and conquests, which may be best described as the expansion of the German and Slavonic people, began in the second century AD. This continued for almost one thousand years, and reshaped the political geography as well as changed the ethnic character of Europe.

The last stage in this process was the expansion of the northern Germans of Scandinavia and Denmark, leading to the settlement of Vikings and Danes in the west and the creation of the Russian state by Swedes in the east. It is impossible to grasp European history without recognizing that the invasions and conquests of the Norsemen which began toward the close of the eighth century were the continuation of the earlier German expansion. It was not until this last stage that Ireland came within range of this general transformation. It was then, in the ninth century, that Teutonic settlements were made on her coasts and a Teutonic kingdom was formed within her borders. Before that time, Ireland had escaped the stress of the political ramblings in Europe.

But four centuries earlier, a force of another kind drew Ireland into union with the continent and made her a part of the Roman world. Still politically aloof at that time, and still impervious to the influence of higher social organization, the island was swept into the spiritual federation which—through the actions of the Emperor Constantine (early fourth century)—had become closely identified with the Roman state. This was what the Roman Empire did for Ireland, not directly or designedly, but automatically, one might say, through the circumstances of its geographical position. The foundation of a church in Ireland was not accomplished until the very hour when the Empire was beginning to fall gradually asunder in the west; and so it happened that when Europe was acquiring a new form and feature in the fifth century, the establishment of the Christian faith in the outlying island appeared as a distinct, though modest, part of the general transformation. Ireland, too, has its small place in the great changes of that era.

To understand the conversion of Ireland, we must take it first as an episode in the history of Europe, glancing at the general conditions of the early propagation of the Christian idea. It is difficult to determine how much Christianity owes its growth and early vitality to the Roman Empire; we can hardly imagine what the rate and mode of its progress through southern and eastern Europe would

The Roman Empire in Britain before Patrick

The Roman Empire may not have extended its reach into Ireland in any coherent fashion before Patrick, but it certainly had done so in Britain. In fact, the land was hotly contested in the generations before Patrick. "Towards the end of the third century, Britain was the center of an imperial crisis. An admiral, Marcus Aurelius Carausius, set himself up as 'Emperor of Western Rome' ca. 286 and minted coins in London. Equipped with a fleet he drove off Saxon pirates from the British shores. He died in 293 and was replaced by another usurper, Allectus. The emperor Constantius Chlorus finally defeated Allectus and recaptured Britain. He restored the economy and protected the coast with a series of forts" (Ashe, note for illustration 17).

A full-page ornament from The Book of Kells, illustrating
the arrest of Christ in Matthew, chapter 26.

have been if those lands had not been united and organized by the might of Rome. It is perhaps not an exaggeration to say that the existence of the empire was a condition of the success of a universal religion in Europe. And it is assuredly true that—even though the Roman government spent 250 years treating Christianity as the one foreign religion not to be tolerated by the state—the faith was more than compensated by the facilities of steady and safe intercourse and communication, which helped the new idea to travel and enabled its preachers and adherents to organize their work and keep in constant touch with each other.

We cannot say exactly how the faith spread in the west; in many ways, the steps of its progress are entirely hidden from us. However, we can mark some stages in the process. We know, for instance, that there were communities in Gaul organized in the second century, and others in Britain at the end of the third. But in neither of these countries did the religion begin to spread widely until after its official recognition by the Emperor Constantine. At the end of the fourth century there were still large districts of Gaul, especially in the Belgic provinces, which were entirely heathen. This sets Gaul and Britain apart from the growth of the faith on the Spanish peninsula. There, Christianity made such rapid strides, and the Spaniards adapted it so skillfully to their pagan habits, that before the time of Constantine, Spain had become, throughout its length and breadth, a Christian land.

The first duty of the bishops of Gaul and Britain, if they undertook any missionary work, was to extend their faith in the parts of their provinces that were still heathen. But there were also several occasions when the religion spread not as a result of missionary zeal, but through the means of Christian captives carried off as slaves. An important part was played by captives in diffusing the knowledge of the Christian religion of the late Roman Empire. For example, the conversion of the kingdom of Eastern Iberia is striking. The story that it became Christian during the reign of Constantine through the bond-slave Nino rests on good evidence. Nino is still revered there—in present-day southern and eastern Georgia—as the "enlightener and equal to the apostles." But even if the tale is not accepted literally, its existence illustrates the important part Christian captives played in the diffusion of their creed.

More about Nino

St. Nino was born sometime around AD 300 and died around 340. Very little is known about her for certain, but she was likely born in Cappadocia, which was then a Roman province. She eventually found her way to Eastern Iberia (to be differentiated from the Iberian peninsula) and is credited with converting Nana, the queen of Georgia, and eventually also her pagan husband, King Mirian III of Iberia.

Similarly, just as captives played a part in the diffusion of Christian faith, so did foreign soldiers. Once they enlisted in the army of the empire, they often came under the influence of Christianity in their garrison stations, and by the time they returned home beyond the frontier, they carried the faith with them.

Merchants and other traveling workers in commerce must have had a similar effect. However, commercial relationships and conditions in ancient and medieval history are among the most difficult to realize because ancient and medieval writers rarely thought to describe them. The foundation of the church in Abyssinia, however, provides one salient example of the part that merchants (as well as captives) played.

A party of Greek explorers was sailing in southern seas when they landed on the coast of Abyssinia. They were slaughtered by natives, with the exception of two youths who were spared to become personal slaves of the king. One of the youths served the king as cupbearer, the other, whose name was Frumentius, as secretary. After the king's death his son's education was entrusted to these two men. Eventually, Frumentius used his influence to help the Roman merchants who traded with Abyssinia to found a Christian church. Afterwards, although Frumentius was permitted to return to his own country, he resolved to dedicate his life to the propagation of Christianity in Abyssinia instead. He was consecrated as bishop of Axum, the capital city of Abyssinia, by St. Athanasius at Alexandria.

Up to the sixth century, the extension of the faith into barbarian territories was not due to direct efforts or deliberate design on the part of the church, so much as it was to chapters of "accidents" which arose through the relations, hostile and pacific, of the empire with its neighbors. The "missions" to the Gentiles were, in practice, limited by the church to the Roman world, although the heads of the church were always ready to recognize, welcome, and affiliate Christian communities that might be planted on barbarian ground by the accidents of private enterprise.

It is important to note, here, the enormous prestige the Roman Empire possessed in the minds of the barbarian people who dwelled beyond it. The observant student who follows the history of the expansion of Germany with care, as well as the strange process by which the German kingdoms were established within the empire in western Europe, is struck at every step by the profound respect the barbarians evinced for the empire and the Roman name throughout all their hostilities and injuries. While they were unconsciously dismembering it, they believed in its impregnable stability. Europe without the empire was unimaginable. The dominion of Rome seemed to them part of the universal order, as eternal as the great globe itself. If we take into account this immeasurable reverence for Rome, which is one of the governing psychical facts in the history of the "wandering of the nations," we can discern what prestige a religion would acquire for neighboring peoples when it became the religion of the Roman people and the Roman state, as it did under Constantine.

Imagine with what different eyes the barbarians must have regarded Christianity when it was a forbidden and persecuted doctrine and when it was raised in the fourth century to be a state religion. At once, it acquired a claim on their attention; it was no longer merely one among many rival doctrines current in the empire. Considerations of political advantage came in, and political motives could sway barbarians no less than Constantine himself in determining their attitude

"Christian" Nations?

Many nations in history have taken pride in their status as a "Christian" nation. In most cases, these claims reach back to the work of an original missionary or religious group who evangelized the country. A scholar of Russian religious history explains the process of converting heathen practices in the following way, which shows parallels to how many Irish feel about the work of Patrick in Ireland: "All Christian nations must be 'twice-born,' but since Grace transforms nature rather than destroys it, they carry deep within them traces of their heathen past. The process of transformation is never complete. In the most civilized of modern peoples there are survivals of the prehistoric ages, now degraded to the rank of superstitions or 'folklore'" (Fedotov, 3).

to a religious creed. And the fact that the Christian God was the God of that great empire was in itself a persuasive argument in its favor. Could a people find any more powerful protector than the deity who was worshiped and feared by the greatest "nation" on earth?

So it seemed to the Burgundians, for instance, who embraced the Roman religion, we are told, because they conceived that "the God of the Romans is a strong helper to those who fear him." The simple barbarians did not reason too inquisitively. It did not occur to them, for instance, that the Eternal City had achieved her greatness and built her empire under the auspices of Jupiter and Mars. There can be little doubt that, if the step taken by Constantine had been postponed for a hundred years, we would not find the Goths and the Vandals professing Christianity at the beginning of the fifth century.

Despite all of these tendencies among the independent neighbors of the Roman Empire, Ireland occupies a singular place (together with the Isle of Man) as the only part of the Celtic world which had not been gathered under the scepter of Rome. Nevertheless, this island was not separate and aloof from Europe. We have lately come to realize the frequency and prevalence of intercourse by sea before historical records began. Hundreds and hundreds of years before the Homeric poems were created, the lands of the Mediterranean were bound together by maritime communication. The same is true of the northern seas at a later period. It would be absurd to suppose that the Celtic conquerors of Britain burned their ships when they reached the island shores and cut themselves off from intercourse with the mainland from which they had crossed. And we may be sure that it was not they who first established regular communications. The pre-Celtic peoples of south Britain knew the waterways to the coasts of the continent. The intimate connection of the Celts of Britain with their kinsfolk across the channel is amply attested in Caesar's history of the conquest of Gaul. Ireland was somewhat further, but not by far.

Relations between Ireland and Britain were inevitable from ancient days through mere proximity, and there is no doubt that regular communication was also maintained with Gaul and Spain. It is highly significant that, during the Celtic period, Roman geographers regarded Ireland as midway between Spain and Britain, a conception which seems to point unmistakably to direct intercourse between Irish and Spanish ports. Irish trade with the empire was noticed by Tacitus, the Roman historian, and in the second century, Ptolemy offers an account of the island which, even though undecipherable in parts, can be judged to be based upon genuine information.

From the very outset of Roman rule of Britain, the question was considered whether Ireland should be occupied or not. A general of Domitian thought the conquest ought to be attempted, but the government decided against his opinion. Why not annex it? After the time of Augustus, no additions were made to Roman dominion except under the stress of political necessity. Britain was annexed by the generals of

Certain Roman Emperors . . .

Bury mentions several Roman emperors:

Julius: Imperator Gaius Julius Caesar Divus; emperor from 49–44 BC. The emperor assassinated by Brutus on the Ides of March.

Augustus: Gaius Julius Caesar Octavianus; ruled from 27 BC–AD 14. The originator of *Pax Romana*.

Claudius: Tiberius Claudius Caesar Augustus Germanicus; emperor from AD 41–54.

Domitian: Titus Flavius Domitianus; emperor from AD 81–96.

Claudius for the same reason that prompted Julius to invade it—political necessity, arising from the dangerously close bonds which united the Britons with the Gauls. In the case of Ireland there were apparently no such pressing considerations. This explanation also accords with the fact that until the middle of the fourth century the Irish and Scots are not named among the dangerous invaders of the British province. In fact, they are not named at all.

But by the end of the fourth century, Christians found their way to the Irish shores. There was regular intercourse with Britain, Gaul, and Spain, and there were Irish settlements in southwest Britain providing a highroad for the new creed to travel. Also, the great invasion in the middle of the fourth century—which will be discussed in the next chapter—must have conveyed Christian captives to Ireland. In the conversion of Ireland, as elsewhere, captives played the part of missionaries.

It will not, then, surprise us that by the fifth century men were going forth from Ireland to be trained in Christian theology. It will not astonish us to learn that Christian communities existed which were ripe for organization, and that the religion was penetrating the house of the high-kings. We will also see reasons for supposing that the Latin alphabet had already made its way to Ireland by the fifth century, and the reception of an alphabet generally means the reception of other influences from the same source.

CHAPTER THREE
How Patrick Came to Ireland

The conversion of Ireland to Christianity has, as we have seen, a place among the many changes that were part of the new Europe of the fifth century. The beginnings of the work had been noiseless and dateless, due to fortunate circumstances and the obscure zeal of mostly nameless pioneers; but it was organized and established, so that it could never be undone, primarily by the efforts of one man, a Roman citizen of Britain who devoted his life to the task.

His Childhood

The child who was destined to play this part in the shaping of a new Europe was born before the close of the fourth century, perhaps in the year AD 389. His father, Calpurnius, was a Britain. Like all free subjects of the empire, he was a Roman citizen, and like his father Potitus before him, he had a Roman name.

Calpurnius belonged to the middle class of landowners, and was a decurion, or member, of the municipal council of a Roman town. His home was in a village named Bannaventa, but we cannot identify its locality with any certainty. The only Bannaventa that we know with certainty lay near Daventry, but this position doesn't agree with the ancient tradition that the village of Patrick's father was close to the western sea. Muirchu, Patrick's earliest biographer, indicates that the place was near the Irish Channel, which makes sense in that it accords with the circumstances of the capture of Patrick; but of course, it

41

is also possible that the Irish invaders might have penetrated to Northamptonshire. The village must have been in the neighborhood of a town possessing a municipal council of decurions; but this does not mean that it was a large town, with the rank of a *colonia*, like Gloucester, or of a *municipium*, like St. Albans, for smaller Roman towns technically known as *praefecturae, fora,* and *conciliabula* might also be managed by municipal councils. There seems to be no reason to doubt that Bannaventa is the name of the home of Calpurnius and Patrick, but there was most likely another Bannaventa near the sea coast.

To be a decurion of the governing council of a Roman town in Calpurnius's day was an unenviable dignity. Every landowner in a municipality who did not belong to the class of senators was obliged to be a decurion, provided that he owned at least sixteen acres. It was on these landowners that the chief burden of imperial taxation fell. They were known as "the sinews of the republic."

Decurions were bound to deliver to the imperial officials the amount of tax levied on their entire community; it was their duty both to collect the tax and to assess the proportion payable by each individual proprietor. In the fourth century, while the class of great landed proprietors (who were mainly senators and entirely free from municipal obligations) was increasing, the class of small landowners was diminishing in numbers and declining in prosperity. This decline progressed rapidly, and the imperial laws which sought to arrest it suggest an appalling picture of economic decay and hopeless misery throughout the provinces. The evils of perverse legislation were aggravated by the corruption and tyranny of the treasury officials, which the emperors, with the best intentions, seemed powerless to prevent. As a result, people devised and sought all possible means of escaping from the sad fate of a decurion's dignity. Many a harassed taxpayer abandoned his land, surrendered his freedom, and became a laborer on the estate of a rich landlord to escape the miseries of a decayed decurion's life. We even find the Emperor Maxentius punishing Christians by promoting them to the dignity of a decurion in the early fourth century.

It is unknown to us whether the municipal classes in Britain suffered as cruelly as their brethren in other parts of the empire. The history of this island throughout the last century of Roman rule is almost a blank. It would be hazardous to draw any inferences from the agricultural prosperity of Britain, whose cornfields sometimes supplied the Roman legions on the Rhine with their daily bread. But it is possible, for all we know, that members of the British municipalities may have enjoyed a less dreary lot than the downtrodden decurions of other provinces.

There was one class of decurions that seems to have caused the emperors considerable perplexity. It was those who, whether from a genuine religious motive or in order to shirk the municipal burdens, took orders in the Christian church. A pagan emperor like Julian the Apostate (d. 363) had no scruple in recalling them sternly to their civil duties, but Christian emperors found it difficult to assert such a principle. They had to sustain the curial system at all costs and yet avoid giving offense to the church. Theodosius the Great (Roman Emperor from 375–95) laid down that the estates of decurions who had become presbyters or deacons before a certain year should be exempt from municipal obligations, but that those who had taken order after that year should forfeit their lands to the state. He qualified this law, however, by a later enactment which provided that if the presbyter or deacon had a son who was not in orders the son might keep the paternal property and perform the accompanying duties.

Two Themes in Irish History

Occupation (by the Anglo-Saxons, French, Vikings, and others) and desertion (waves of emigration that were more like fleeing a burning ship than seeking opportunity) are two themes that dominate Irish history. Irish fiction has always been characterized by a certain self-consciousness focused on the uncertainty of Ireland's roots, occupations, and inherited Christianity. "What does it mean to be truly Irish?" is a persistent theme. Contemporary Irish novelist Anne Enright's newest novel, *The Gathering*, is both typical and therapeutic in this sense: the main character of Veronica finds redemption for her troubles in Ireland itself—after journeying to England and then back again.

Patrick's father, Calpurnius, belonged to this class of decurions who had sought ordination. This was the period of time in the history of the Catholic Church before the principle of celibacy had been generally applied to the clergy. It was in answer to an appeal from a Spanish bishop that Pope Siricius wrote his decretal of AD 385, laying down the necessity of celibacy for all clergy in the western churches. Yet, it was much later that the Gallic councils found it necessary to legislate against them. Calpurnius was a Christian deacon and his father before him had been a presbyter. And it would seem as if they had found it feasible to combine their spiritual with their worldly duties. In any case, we may assume that the property remained in the family and was not forfeited to the state.

Whether the burdens laid upon them from Milan or Constantinople were heavy or light, Calpurnius and his neighbors in the northern island were keenly conscious that the rule of their Roman lords had its compensations. For Britain was bothered by three bold and ruthless foes: the northern frontier was threatened by the Picts of Caledonia; the western shores dreaded the descents of the Gaels and Scots of Ireland; and the south and east were exposed to those Saxon freebooters who were ultimately to conquer the island. Against these enemies, ever watching for a favorable opportunity to spoil their rich neighbor, the Roman garrison was usually a strong and sure protection for the peaceful Britons. But favorable opportunities sometimes came.

Potitus, at least, if not Calpurnius, must have shared in the agonies that Britain felt in those two terrible years when she was attacked on all sides by Pict, by Scot, and by Saxon, when Theodosius the Elder, the great emperor's father, had to come in haste and use all his strength to deliver the province from the barbarians. In the valley of the Severn the foes whom the Britons dreaded were Irish freebooters, and surely in those years their pirate crafts sailed up the river and brought death and ruin to many.

Theodosius defeated Saxon, Pict, and Scot, and it would seem that he pursued the Scots across the sea, driving them back to their own shores. The court poet of his grandson sings how icebound Hiverne wept for the heaps of her slain children. After this, the land had peace for a space. Serious and thoroughgoing measures were taken for its defense, and an adequate army was left under a capable commander. People could breathe freely once more; but the breathing space lasted less than fifteen years.

The usurpation of the tyrant Emperor Maximus (d. 388) brought new calamities to Britain. Maximus came to power in the western Roman Empire by the will of the soldiers, who were dissatisfied with the government of Gratian (d. 383). And if the provincials approved of this rash coup, they perhaps hoped that

Maximus would be content to exercise his authority only in their own island. If Maximus were to desire a more spacious field for his ambition, it would have been difficult for him, a usurper, to maintain his power, with the adhesion of Britain alone, against the power of the lord of the west. The best chance of success would be for the tyrant to win Gaul. And so Maximus crossed the English Channel, taking the army, or at least a part of it, with him. His own safety was at stake; he did not worry about the safety of the province he left behind; whatever forces he left on the shores and on the northern frontier were unequal to the task of protecting the island against the foes who were ever waiting for a propitious hour to pounce on their prey. Bitterly were the Britons destined to rue the day when Maximus was invested with the purple.

Denuded of defenders, they had again to bear the invasions of Pict, Saxon, and Scot. Rescue came after the fall of Maximus, and the son of their former defender, the emperor Theodosius the Great, empowered his most trusted general, Stilicho, to make all necessary provision for the defense of the remote province. The enemies seem to have escaped, safe and sated, from the shores of Britain before the return of the army. But Britain, says a contemporary poet, was well-nigh done to death.

The distress of these years must have been felt by Calpurnius and his household. It was probably just before or just after this new period of security had begun that a son was born to Calpurnius and his wife, Concessa (ca. AD 389). It may have been the habit of native provincials to give their children two names, a Latin name, which stamped them as Romans, as well as a British name, which would naturally be used in home life. Calpurnius called his son Patricius. But if Patricius spoke the Brythonic tongue as a child in the home of his father and mother, he bore the name of Sucat. In this way, he may have been double-named, as was the apostle Paul, who bore a Roman as well as a Jewish name from his youth up. (There is no evidence that the name Paul was adopted or new at his conversion.) But another Roman name, Magonus, is also ascribed to Patrick; possibly, his full style—as it would appear in the town registry when he should come of age to exercise the rights of a citizen—was Patricius Magonus Sucatus.

As the son of a deacon, Patrick was educated in the Christian faith and was taught the Christian scriptures. And we may be sure that he was brought up to feel deep reverence for the empire in which he was born a freeman and citizen, and to regard Rome as the mighty bulwark of the world. This feeling comes out in his writings, and it may have been strengthened by the experiences of his life. Peaceful people in Britain in those days could have imagined no more terrible disaster than to be sundered from the empire. Rome was the symbol of peace and civilization, and to Rome they passionately clung. The worst thing they had to dread from year to year was that the Roman army would be summoned to meet some sudden need in another province.

Patrick's Real Name?

The *Catholic Encyclopedia* doesn't even address the subject of Patrick's real name, and many biographers don't touch on it either. It seems to be an almost trivial concern given that the first two words of Patrick's book *Confession* are, "I, Patrick . . . " Given the relative lack of sure information we have about St. Patrick, it is remarkable to hear a modern biographer still say, "He was . . . the only ancient Briton whom we really know" (Thompson, xi). The survival of Patrick's own writings is the sole reason we know more (relatively speaking) about him than about any other ancient resident of the British isles.

But as Patrick grew up, the waves were already gathering, to close slowly over the island, and to sweep the whole of western Europe. The great Theodosius died, and his two feeble successors slumbered in Milan and Constantinople while the barbarians were pressing at the gates, armed and ready, impressed by Rome's majesty and hungry for the spoils. Hardly was Theodosius at rest in his tomb when Greece was laid waste by the Goths and Athens tumbled at the presence of Alaric. But still, the people of the empire did not yet realize the strange things that were to come, and where the menace and the presage would come from.

When the rumor of King Alaric I and his Goths reached the homesteads of Britain, it must have struck their ears as a thing far off, a trouble with which they could easily have no part. And the danger that lurked for the empire was muffled and disguised. Alaric was a Goth, but at the same time he was an imperial general, a master of soldiers, a servant of the Roman state, profoundly loyal to the empire, the integrity of which he was undermining.

A few years later Britain was startled by sudden events: Alaric and his Goths entered Italy itself. Emperor Honorius was trembling on his throne, and the armies of the west had to hurry to defend him. The message came from Stilicho—the general on whose strength and skill the safety of western Europe had depended in those years—and one legion from Briton obeyed the summons to come to Italy. The islanders must have once again been sick at heart, as they left Briton for the continent, in expectation of the daily danger of assault from their old enemies at home.

Those enemies were wide awake, in fact, and they rose up to take advantage of the favorable circumstances. At this point we encounter an Irish king whose name is famous in the obscure history of his own land. King Niall was the high-king of Ireland in the days of the rebellion of Magnus Maximus, and may possibly have joined in the marauding expeditions that vexed Britain during those years. His deeds are enveloped in legend, but the exalted notion that his countrymen formed of his prowess is expressed in the vain tale that he invaded Gaul and conquered as far as the Alps. To the annals of the empire, King Niall is as unknown as the princelings of remotest Scythia, but in Britain his name must have been familiar. It seems that he died out of his own country, was slain by the hand of a fellow countryman, and that he met his death "by the Sea of Wight," according to one of the Irish annals. If the date assigned to the king's death, AD 405, is roughly correct, then this last hosting of King Niall in Britain happened before the Roman army had finally left the island, but during the disorders that preceded its departure.

His Capture

We will never stray too far from the direct relevance of these events to the home life of St. Patrick, and in this case, the life of his father, Calpurnius. It may have been during this crisis in the history of Britain that the events of Patrick's capture occurred. These events obviously shaped the entire life of the son of Calpurnius, who had now reached the age of sixteen in his home near the western sea.

A fleet of Irish freebooters came to the coasts or riverbanks in the neighborhood seeking plunder and loading their vessels with captives. Patrick was at his father's farmstead, and was one of the victims. Menservants and maidservants were taken, but his parents escaped; perhaps they were not there, or perhaps the pirates could not carry more than a certain number of slaves, and chose the young.

This is how Patrick, in his seventeenth year, was carried into captivity in Ireland—"to the ultimate places of the earth," as he says himself, as if Ireland were severed by half the globe from Britain. The phrase shows how thoroughly, how touchingly Roman was Patrick's geographical view. The Roman Empire was the world, and everything outside its fringe was in darkness, the ultimate places of the earth.

CHAPTER FOUR
Captivity and Escape

We know very little of what happened to Patrick during his captivity in Ireland, but the little that we do know is more immediate and authentic than our knowledge of any other episode of his life—because it comes from his own pen. But at the outset we encounter a puzzling contradiction between Patrick's own words and the tradition that was long current in Ireland as to the place of his bondage.

When the boats of his captors reached their haven, Patrick was led—so we should conclude from his own story—across the island into the kingdom of Connaught, to serve a master in the very furthest parts of the "ultimate land." His master dwelled near the wood of Fochlad, "near to the western sea," in northwestern Connaught, to this day a wild and desolate land, although the forest has long since been cleared away. The wood of Fochlad may have stretched over Mayo to the western promontory of Murrisk. There, we should perhaps suppose, close to Crochan Aigli, the mountain that has been immemorially associated with Patrick's name, the British slave served his master for six years.

From his own words, it is certain that Patrick served his master near the forest of Fochlad. Nevertheless, some traditions place him in a more distant part of Ireland, in Pictish soil near the eastern coast of Ulster. There, in the lands east of Lough Neagh, the old race that was driven eastward from central Ulster still held out. In the extreme north were the Scots, and in the south were the Picts. The small land of the Scots was known as Dalriada, and the larger land of the Picts as Dalaradia.

There, it was believed and recorded, Patrick served a master whose name was Miliucc. His lands and his homestead were in northern Dalaradia, and Patrick herded his droves of pigs on the mountain of Miss. The name of this mountain remains unchanged, although when joined with *sliabh*, the Gaelic word for "mountain," it is slightly disguised. Not really lofty, and not visible at a distance of many miles—nevertheless, when you come within its range, Mount Miss dominates the whole scene and produces the impression of a massive mountain. Its curious, striking shape, like an inverted bowl, round and wide-brimmed, exercises a charm on the eye and haunts the viewer in the valley of Braid, like the pediment of a temple follows one about in the plain of Athens.

We may attempt to reconcile the contradiction between the forest of Fochlad and the valley of Braid by assuming that Patrick changed masters. Perhaps, having dwelled at first in the west, he was then sold to another master in Dalaradia? But no, because his own description of his bondage does not support this sort of conjecture. The

Two Sacred Places in the History of St. Patrick

As Bury concludes, St. Patrick spent six years of his young life near the forest of Fochlad, and the small mountain called Crochan Aigli, or "Eagle Mountain." The latter has since been renamed Croagh Patrick, or Mount Patrick; at 2,510 feet tall, it sits close to the town of Westport in County Mayo, and is visited by tens of thousands of pilgrims each year, particularly on the last Sunday of July, when many of them climb the mountain barefoot. It is said that Patrick fasted for forty days on the mountain at some point during his lifetime, and from its summit drove the snakes out of Ireland. The summit of Croagh Patrick has probably been a recognized sacred site since before the arrival of Christianity in Ireland.

simplest solution seems to be a frank rejection of the story that connects his captivity with Mount Miss in the land of the Picts.

The Schooling of Hardship

While he ate the bitter bread of bondage in a foreign land, a profound spiritual change came over Patrick. He had never given much thought to his religion, but now that he was a thrall among strangers, "the Lord," Patrick says, "opened the sense of my unbelief." The ardor of religious emotion, "the love and fear of God," so fully consumed his soul that in a single day or night he would offer a hundred prayers. And he describes himself, in woodland or on mountainside, rising from his bed before dawn and going out to pray in hail, or rain, or snow.

Thus the years of his bondage were also the years of his conversion, and he looked back upon this stage in his spiritual development as the most important and critical in his life.

But still, he was homesick, and he was too young to abandon hope of deliverance and escape from the wild outland into which fate had cast him. He longed and hoped, and we may be sure that he prayed, to win his way back within the borders of the Roman Empire. His waking

In Patrick's Own Words . . .

"After I came to Ireland, I was daily tending sheep, and I prayed frequently during the day, and the love of God, and His faith and fear, increased in me more and more, and the spirit was stirred. In one single day I have said as many as a hundred prayers, and in the night nearly the same. I remained in the woods, and on the mountain, even before the dawn. I was roused to prayer in snow and ice and rain, and I felt no injury from it; nor was there any laziness in me, as I see now, because the spirit was fervent within me. And there one night I heard a voice, while I slept, saying to me: 'You do well to fast. Fasting, you shall soon return to your native land.' And again, after a very short time, I heard a response, saying to me: 'Behold, your ship is ready.' And the place was far off, perhaps two hundred miles away; I had never been there before, and I didn't know any one who lived there. But I fled, and left the man with whom I had been six years, and I came in the strength of the Lord, who directed my way for good. I feared nothing until I arrived at that ship." (from his *Confession*)

hopes came back to him at night as responsive voices in his dreams. He heard a voice that said to him in his sleep, "You do well to fast. Fasting, you shall soon return to your native land." And another night it said, "Behold, your ship is ready." Patrick took these dream voices for divine intimations and they heartened him to make an attempt at escape. But escape was not easy, and was beset with many perils.

The port where he might hope to find a foreign vessel was about 180 miles from his master's house. Patrick, in describing his escape, does not name the port, but we may conjecture that it was Inverdea, at the mouth of the stream which is now called the Vartry, reaching the sea near the town of Wicklow. The reason for conjecturing Wicklow is that it seems to have been a port where foreign ships might be looked for; both Palladius and Patrick later landed there. Patrick ascribes the resolution of attempting this long flight, with the danger of falling into the hands of some other master—or of being overtaken by his own—to the promptings of a higher will than his own.

He escaped all of these dangers and reached the port, where he knew no one. The ship of his dreams was there, and was about to sail. It was a ship of traders; their cargo was on board and part of the cargo consisted of dogs, probably Irish wolfhounds. Patrick spoke to some of the crew and made a proposal of service. He was willing to work for his passage to the port to which the vessel was bound. The proposal seems to have been entertained at first, but afterwards the shipmaster objected and said sharply, "No, in no way shall you come with us." The disappointment must have been bitter to Patrick, since safety seemed within his grasp. But he turned away from the mariners to seek lodging elsewhere. As he went and prayed, and before he finished his prayer, he heard one of the crew shouting behind him, "Come quickly, for they are calling you!" The shipmaster had been persuaded to forget his objections and Patrick set sail from the shores of Ireland with this rough company.

To what country or race the crew belonged we are not told. We learn only that they were heathen. They wished to enter into some solemn compact of abiding friendship with Patrick, but he refused to be adopted by them. "I would not," he says, using a quaint phrase, "suck their breasts because of the fear of God. Nevertheless I hoped for them that they might come to the faith of Christ, for they were heathen, and for that reason I held on with them."

They sailed for three days before they made land. The name of the coast they reached is hidden from us, and there is something very strange about the whole story. The voyage was clearly uneventful. They were not driven by storm or stress of weather out of their course to some undesired shore. There is nothing in the tale, as Patrick tells it himself, to suggest that the ship did not reach the port to which it was bound. Yet when they landed, they had to make their way through a desert and journeyed for twenty-eight days in all. The food supply ran short, and at last starvation threatened; many of their dogs were exhausted and left to die on the wayside. Then the shipmaster said to Patrick, "Now, Christian, you say that your God is great and almighty. Why then don't you pray for us? For we are in danger of starvation and there is little chance we will come upon help."

And Patrick, in the spirit of the missionary, replied, "Nothing is impossible to the Lord, my God. Turn to him honestly, that he may send you food in your path this day until you are filled, for God has plenty in all places." Soon afterwards, a drove of pigs appeared on the road and the starving wayfarers killed many of them, resting there for two nights, and were refreshed. They were as ready as Patrick himself to believe that the appearance of the swine was a miraculous answer to his prayer, and he won high esteem in their eyes.

As Patrick slept in that place, his body satisfied with a plenteous meal after long privation, he dreamed a dream that he remembered vividly as long as he lived. He dreamed that a great stone fell on top of him and he couldn't move his limbs. Then he called upon St. Elias, the great prophet Elijah, and the beams of the rising sun awoke him, the feeling of heaviness fell away. Patrick regarded this nightmare as a temptation from Satan, and imagined that Christ had come to his aid. The incident has a ridiculous side, but it shows the intense religious excitement of Patrick at this time in his life, ready to see in the most trivial occurrence a direct interposition from heaven. And we must remember how in those days dreams were universally invested with a certain mystery and dread.

For nine more days Patrick and his companions traveled through deserted places, but were not in want of food or shelter. On the tenth, they finally came upon other men. By this time, Patrick had no desire or need to stay any longer with the ship's crew, but he heard a divine voice in another dream answering his thoughts, saying, "You shall remain with them two months." This dream naturally guided him in choosing the time of his escape. At the end of two months he succeeded in releasing himself from his masters.

In his description of this strange adventure he leaves us to divine the geography, for he relates the events as if they had happened in some nameless land beyond the borders of the known world. However, the circumstances enable us to determine that the ship made for the coast of Gaul. It can be shown that its destination was not Britain, and Gaul is the only other land that could have been reached in three days or thereabouts. The aim of the traders with the Irish dogs must have been to reach southern Europe, and the place of disembarkation would naturally have been Nantes or Bordeaux. The story of the long faring through a wilderness might be taken to illustrate the condition of western and southwestern Gaul during that period.

Patrick and his companions reached land three days after they left the coast of Ireland, so our choice of geography lies between Britain and Gaul. The data do not support Britain. We cannot imagine what inland part of Britain they could have wished to reach that would have necessitated a journey of twenty-eight days.

Considerable regions of Gaul were a desolate wilderness, according to contemporary evidence from AD 408–416. About the time that Patrick's adventures happened, Gallic poets were writing heartbreaking descriptions of the desolation that had been brought upon this country by the great invasion of Vandals and Sueves and other barbarous peoples. Vandals, Sueves, and Alans entered Gaul at the end of 406 and remained in the land, devastating, slaying, and burning until 409, the year in which they crossed the Pyrenees to find homes in Spain. The extent of their ravages is indicated by St. Jerome in a letter of AD 411, in which he mentions the devastation of Aquitania, Lugdunensis, and Narbonensis, and the destruction of Mainz, Rheims, and Speyer. Strong castles, walled cities, sings one poet, could not escape; the hands of the barbarians reached even lonely lodges in dismal wilds and the very caves in the hills. "If the whole ocean," cries another, "had poured its water into the fields of Gaul, its vast waves would have spared more than the invaders."

But even in the exceptional conditions of the time, it is surprising that a party, starting from a port on the west coast and traveling to the Mediterranean, would have walked for four weeks without seeing a human abode and in dire peril of starvation. We must suppose that they deliberately and carefully avoided beaten roads, and perhaps made considerable halts, in order to avoid encounters with roaming bands of the Teutonic barbarians.

Though Patrick did not mention the scene of his journey in the narrative that he left behind, he used to tell his disciples how he had "the fear of God as a guide in his journey through Gaul and Italy." This confirms the conclusion to which other evidence points, that Gaul was the destination of the crew, and also intimates that he traveled with his companions through Gaul to Italy. It was in Italy, then, we must suppose, that he succeeded in escaping from them.

When Patrick described this episode, he was an old man. He rigidly omitted all details that did not bear upon his special purpose in writing. The whole tale of his captivity and escape, undefined or vaguely defined by landmarks or seamarks, as if the places of the adventures had no name or lay beyond the range of all human charts, is designed to display the exclusively spiritual significance of those experiences. That the land of his captivity was Ireland was indeed significant; but otherwise, names of people and places were of no concern and were allowed to drop away. In reviewing this critical period of his life, Patrick reproduces the select incidents as they impressed him at the moment, contributing, as he believed, to his own spiritual development or illustrating the wonderful ways that heaven had dealt with him.

CHAPTER FIVE

Sojourn in Gaul and Back to Britain

Patrick did not tell us where, or in what circumstances, he parted from his companions. He also did not relate his subsequent adventures.

When he found himself free, his first thought must have been to make his way back to his home in Britain. He probably succeeded in escaping from his fellow travelers in Italy, and his easiest way home might, in that case, have been by the coast road through Liguria and Provence to Marseilles. From wherever he started, he seems to have reached the coast of Provence. For here at length, amid perplexing and broken clues, we have a definite trace of his path; here we can fix an episode in his life to a small plot of ground.

In the later part of the fourth century the influence of the Eastern on the Western mind had displayed itself not only in theological thought, but also in the spread of asceticism and the foundation of monastic societies. Men such as Ambrose, Martin of Tours, and Jerome played a significant role in those days. In choosing their lonely dwelling places, the eyes of anchorites did not overlook the little, deserted islands that lay here and there off the coast in the western Mediterranean. Island cloisters studded the coast of Italy "like a necklace" before the end of the fourth century, and soon they began to appear off the coast of Provence. It was perhaps while Patrick was a slave in Ireland that a traveler, weary of the world, came back from the east to his native Gaul, and seeking a spot where he might found a little society of monks who desired to live far from the turmoil of cities, was directed to the uncouth island of Lerinus, which no one had ever tilled or approached because it was infested with snakes. Honoratus took possession of it and reclaimed it for cultivation. Wells were dug, and sweet water flowed "in the midst of the bitterness of the sea." Vines were planted and cells were built, and a little monastic community gathered around Honoratus, destined within a few years to be more illustrious than any of the older island cloisters.

Lerinus is the outermost of the two islands that lie opposite the cape of Cannes, smaller and lower than its fellow Lero, which screens it from view. It is difficult to realize today, as one walks around it and sees a few stones and relics of its ancient monks, that at one time it exercised a great, if unobtrusive, influence in southern Gaul. Its peaceful, sequestered cells, "withdrawn into the great sea," had a wonderful attraction for men who had been shipwrecked in the tumbling world, or who desired unbroken hours for contemplation.

The Lerins Islands
on the French Riviera

The Lerins Islands lie about one half-mile off the shore of the coast of France near Cannes, site of the famous annual film festival on the Riviera. They are frequented by boats from Cannes. The island of Lero (mentioned by Bury), called by the name of Sainte-Marguerite today, was the largest of the islands and the site of a fortress prison made famous by the true story of "the man in the iron mask" during the reign of Louis XIV. The unfortunate man was also held in the Bastille in Paris. The island of Lerinus is the second-largest of the chain and goes by the name Saint-Honorat, today, in honor of the monastery founder, Honoratus, whom Bury speaks of. Honoratus's contemporary, John Cassian, speaks of the monastery there as being "immense" by the year 427.

Patrick found a refuge in the island cloister of Honoratus, and it is on that island that we are first treading on ground we have reason to think he lived for a considerable time. We would like to know the circumstances of his admission to that community; his own picture of the state of his mind enables us to understand how easily he could have been moved by the ascetic attractions of the monastery to interrupt his homeward journey and lead a religious life in the *sacrae solitudines* ("sacred solitude") of Lerinus for a few years.

Among the men of note who sojourned in the monastery in its early days were Hilary, who afterwards became bishop of Arelate; Maximus, who was the second abbot, and then bishop of Reii; Lupus, who subsequently held the see of Trecasses; Vincentius, who taught and wrote in the cloister; and Eucherius, who composed, among other works, a treatise in praise of the hermit's life. Eucherius had a hut built for himself after the death of his wife, Galla, far away from the rest of the brotherhood, in the larger island of Lero. It was remembered how one day Honoratus sent a messenger across in a boat with a letter on a wax tablet, and Eucherius, seeing the abbot's writing, said, "To the wax you have restored its honey."

As the monastic spirit grew and spread, many strangers set their faces to Lerinus, hoping, as people hoped greatly in those days, that "the kingdom of heaven has suffered violence, and the violent take it by force" (Mt. 11:12). Among those who joined the new society was Faustus, a

More about Eucherius

St. Eucherius of Lyon (ca. 380–ca. 449) was one of the most interesting figures of late antiquity. In his life as a hermit, lived after he had been the bishop of Lyons, Eucherius consulted with John Cassian who had chronicled a sort of "greatest teachings" of the ascetics of the eastern deserts and wildernesses in Egypt and Syria and Palestine. Eucherius sought to live as these others were living, but back in Gaul in the Lerins islands. And he continued to study and learn, talking with other great ascetics who were devoted to learning from texts. He joined a distinguished category of hermit/ascetic/scholar —like St. Jerome had been before him. The treatise "in praise of the hermit's life," mentioned by Bury, was indeed *De laude eremi* written for Bishop Hilary of Arles sometime around 428. His work with texts was renowned to the point of being praised by Erasmus during the Renaissance.

compatriot of Patrick. But it is unknown whether or not he was at Lerins at this time; perhaps he was still only a child, for we first hear of him in the abbotship of Maximus, who succeeded Honoratus in AD 426. Faustus himself, then, succeeded Maximus in 433. Faustus had enjoyed an education that Patrick never had. He was a student of ancient philosophy and a master of style. Afterwards, he was the valued friend and correspondent of the greatest man of letters of that century, Sidonius Apollinaris. Patrick must have seemed crude and rustic, by comparison, to his fellow countrymen, when they met at Lerins. And yet today, the name of Faustus has passed out of our memory, while Patrick's is familiar in the households of western Christendom.

The years that Patrick spent at Lerins exercised an abiding influence on him. He was brought under the spell of the monastic ideal; and although his life was not to be sequestered, but out in the active world of people, monastic societies became a principal and indispensable element in his idea of a Christian church. It is doubtful that, during these years of seclusion, he was stirred even faintly by the idea of devoting himself to the work of spreading Christianity in the barbarous land associated with his slavery and shame. But he was profoundly convinced that during the years of his bondage he had been held as in the palm of God's hand; whatever hopes or ambitions he may have cherished in his boyhood must have been driven from his heart by the stress of his experience, and in such a frame of mind the instinct of a man of that age was to turn to a religious life. At Lerins, he may have desired to remain a monk. But there were energies and feelings in him that such a life would not have satisfied. At the end of a few years he left the monastery to visit his kinsfolk in Britain, and there he became conscious of the true destiny of his life.

At Home in Britain

When Patrick returned to his old home, his kin welcomed him "as a son." In using this expression, "as a son," Patrick shows that *parentes* was intended to mean kinsfolk, not parents, because it is most likely that his parents

The Monks of Lerins

Many scholars have argued that Patrick's exposure to the monastic life at Lerins was essential to his later work. Also, the monastic character of the Irish Church after Patrick's death—as opposed to a more ecclesiastical character—was probably owing to the saint's disposition and way of leading and teaching. "Honoratus at Lerins founded his monastery frankly after Egyptian models. . . . The monastery proper was thus used for purposes of purgation, and when the monk had arrived at the stage where he was capable of uninterrupted contemplation he retired to the *desert* and lived there as an anchorite. The religious and moral perfection necessary before the monk could aspire to such heights was pursued within the monastery with great zeal. Poverty, chastity, obedience, fasts, vigils, Bible-reading, were practiced as in Egypt. In liturgical prayer, and especially in the possession of beautiful hymns, the monks of Lerins were in advance of the Egyptians. The insular situation of the monastery was of considerable advantage to it in an age of incursions and terrible unrest. . . . Here St. Patrick studied and here he acquired that excellent knowledge of the Holy Scriptures and that solid grounding in Catholic teaching which stood him in good stead when he came to Ireland" (Ryan, 406).

were dead by this time. They implored him to stay and never leave them again. But if he had any thought of yielding to their persuasions, it was dismissed when he became aware, all at once, that the aim of his life was determined. The idea of laboring among the heathen, which may have been gradually, though quite unconsciously, gathering force and secretly winning possession of his brain, suddenly began to take full and sensible shape in his imagination. In a dream, he saw a man standing by his side. He was named Victoricus in the dream. We may be able to suppose that Patrick had made this man's acquaintance while in Gaul and that he was interested in Ireland—but his only appearance in history is in Patrick's dream.

To the dreamer, Victoricus seemed to have come from Ireland, and in his hand he held a bundle of letters.

And he gave me one of these, and I read the beginning of the letter, and it contained "the voice of the Irish." And as I read the beginning of it, I imagined that I heard the voice of the people who were near the wood of Fochlad, near to the western sea. And this was the cry: "We pray you, holy youth, to come and walk among us again as you did before." I was pierced to the heart and could read no more. After that, I woke up.

This is the dreamer's description of his dream. But as the story was told in later days, the cry that pierced his heart was uttered by the young children of Fochlad, and even by children who were still unborn. There is no mention of this in Patrick's words, and yet the tradition betrays a true instinct of the significance of the dream. It brings out more intensely and pathetically how the hopeless condition of the helpless unbaptized, condemned to everlasting punishment by the doctrine of the church, could appeal irresistibly to the empathy of a Christian who held that rigorous doctrine.

This doctrine was closely connected with another question that was agitating western Christendom at this time. And, strange to say, the controversy had been opened by a man of Irish descent. It is possible that, as some claim, Pelagius was born in Ireland, but the evidence points instead to the conclusion that he belonged to an Irish family settled in western Britain. His name surely represents some Irish sea name such as Muirchu, "hound of the sea." While Patrick was serving in Ireland, Pelagius was in Rome, thinking out one of the great problems that has constantly perplexed the meditations of humankind, and he was promulgating a view that arrested the interest or compelled the attention of leaders of theological opinion from York to Carthage, from Carthage to Jerusalem. For some years the Roman Empire echoed with his fame.

Pelagianism is not one of those dull, lifeless heresies that have no more interest than the fact that they once possessed the minds of people long since dead for a short interval of time. During his time, the movement of human thought was confined within the lines of theology, couched in theological language, and the speculations of perpetual human interest centered around theological controversies. The chief and central principle of Pelagius was the recognition of free will as an unalienable property of human nature. In every action a person is free to choose between good and evil, and his choice has not been predetermined by the diety who originally gave to humans that power of choosing. Pelagius regarded free will as the palladium and surrogate of the dignity of human nature. This view logically excluded the doctrine of original sin, inherited from Adam, as well as the doctrine of predestination. It implied that infants are born sinless, and that baptism is not necessary to save them from hell. This thesis struck at the very root of the theory of the "atonement"—at least as the atonement was crudely conceived by the church in dependence on the old Jewish story of the fall of Adam. Pelagius does not seem to have succeeded in really working his theory of human nature into the Christian system, which he otherwise accepted completely, and this was the logical weakness of his position in the theological debate.

Pelagius was not merely a speculator. He was a monk and rigorous about life, and held the practical aim of raising the morality of Christians; his particular view of human nature and "sin" bore directly on this practical aim. For if the purpose of religion is to realize the ideal of holiness and draw people up above the level of commonplace sensual life, to high and heavenly things, then the doctrine of sin should be framed by the church with this view in mind. There was a danger that, if people were taught that they were born evil and impotent to resist it by efforts of their own, then the moral consciousness would be stifled and paralyzed by a belief so dishonoring to humanity. The assertion of the freedom of the will by Pelagius, and his denial of innate sin, represent a reaction of the moral consciousness against the dominance of the religious consciousness.

To the surveyor of the history of humanity, this is the interest that Pelagius holds—an interest that is often obscured in the dust of controversy. He was the champion of human nature, as such, which the Christian church dishonored and branded as essentially depraved in pursuance of its high goals. He was the champion of all the good people who lived "on the outskirts of the world," as people of Irish ancestry would have said, before Jesus was ever born, and of all the noble and sinless pagans, whether they were many or few. This was the merit of Pelagius, to have attempted to rescue the dignity of human nature oppressed by the doctrine of original sin.

Few people deserve more praise from the Celts of Ireland or Britain than Pelagius, for he dared to say that, before Jesus, sinless people had lived on the earth. He was a bold thinker who went out to speak holy words for humanity, and he butted up against the authorities of St. Augustine and St. Jerome. But Pelagius was not fond of fighting; he wished to keep the whole question out of the region of dogma, and allow it to remain a matter of opinion. He never sought to get his own views sanctioned by a council of the church. What interests us is that Pelagius, who was himself originally inspired by Rufinus, stimulated the thinking of thinking people throughout the west, and induced many to modify their views about free will and inherited sin.

The repose of the monastery at Lerins was not immune to this debate, and some of its more notable monks showed afterwards that they had been profoundly influenced by it. Therefore, the subject must have been familiar to Patrick; the doctrine that infants are sinful at their birth and therefore incur the everlasting punishment of the wicked until they are redeemed through the mysterious rite of baptism might have affected his imagination. Nothing could have done more to enliven his concern for the unbaptized people by the western

Patrick and Pelagius

Two recent scholars have specifically disputed this notion of Bury's that Patrick may have had reasons to sympathize with the ideas of Pelagius. "Indeed, there are numerous passages in Patrick's writings that show his deep-rooted belief that his actions are motivated by grace, not by will. . . . If we assume, as most authorities have, that Patrick's *Confessio* was addressed to superiors in Britain at some point in the fifth century, we must allow for the possibility that Patrick was arguing the case for grace and God's irresistible will against the proponents of voluntarism, in other words, against Pelagian sympathizers, or even—if we allow an early date for Patrick's mission—against Pelagian clergy. Surely Patrick's repeated appeal to his utter lack of control in the decision to go to Ireland points in this direction" (Herren/Brown, 82–83).

sea than a vivid realization of this idea.

The self-revealing dream convinced Patrick that he was destined to go as a missionary and helper to Ireland—*ad ultimum terrae*, "to the limit of the world." And yet he felt hesitation and uncertainty, distrusting his own fitness for the enterprise, conscious of the defective education of his youth, and a natural repugnance to return to the land of captivity. His self-questionings and diffidence were in the end overcome by the mastering instinct of his soul. The instinct seemed to speak within him, to his religious imagination, like an inner voice, confirming his purpose. Such experiences happen to people of a certain cast and mold when an impulse, which they can hardly justify when they weigh it in the scales of the understanding, affects them so strongly that it seems to be the objective compulsion or admonition of some external intelligence.

Study at Auxerre and Bishop Germanus

When he was finally convinced of the destination of his life, Patrick probably did not tarry long in Britain, but returned to Gaul in order to prepare himself for carrying out his task. It was unnecessary to train himself, but to win support for his enterprise from influential authorities in the church. Even if Patrick had already been in clerical orders, it would have been the adventure of a wild fanatic, and would have excited general concern, to set sail in the first ship that left the mouth of the Severn for the Irish coast, and, trusting simply in his own zeal and divine protection, set out to convert the heathen of Connaught. This was not the way that Patrick sought to pursue his dream. He knew that, if he was to succeed, he must come with support and resources and fellow workers, accredited and in touch with the Christian communities that already existed in Ireland. He needed theological study and the counsels of men of leading and light, but also material support and official recognition.

At this time, the church of Autissiodorum—which is the old Gallic name for the town of Auxerre, situated on the river Yonne in central France—seems to have already won a high position in northern Gaul through the virtues of its bishop, Amator. But it was soon to win even higher fame through the greater talents of Amator's successor.

Like most towns in Gaul, and unlike most towns in Britain, we know much about the life of Auxerre through all the changes that have come since it was Patrick's home in the reign of Emperors Honorius and Valentinian I. It was Auxerre that Patrick chose as the place of his study. Perhaps he was introduced to Amator by British ecclesiastics. Or, there may have been some special link or intimacy between the church of Auxerre and one of the British sees. There also may be further motives that

When Did Auxilius and Iserninus First Travel to Ireland?

Bury mentions that we do not know the nationality of Auxilius; in fact, scholars seem to be divided on this question. The older view is that he was a Lombard, the Germanic people of northern Europe; but more recent scholars have centered on his being from Italy. Either way, there is no doubt that Auxilius became a missionary to Ireland in AD 403 and died in 459. There is little else that we may presume to know about him, except that he had a famous brother, St. Seachnaill (see chapter 10), who also appears to have accompanied Patrick to Ireland in 432. This, again, is the traditional view, taken by the *Catholic Encyclopedia*, Bury, and many others. More recently, some scholars have argued that St. Seachnaill actually preceded St. Patrick to Ireland by about three years, to assist Palladius, and that Auxilius and Iserninus were first Seachnaill's companions, not Patrick's. See chapter 6 for more on the Palladius vs. Patrick discussion.

factored into Patrick's making his choice. Perhaps some particular interest in Auxerre had been exhibited previously in the Christian communities of Ireland. There is, in fact, evidence that points to the conclusion that Auxerre was a resort of Irish Christians for theological study, before Patrick.

Patrick was ordained a deacon by Bishop Amator before long, and it seems that two other young men were ordained at the same time, who were to help afterwards in the spread of Christianity in Ireland. One of them was a native of southern Ireland; his Irish name was Fith, but he took the name of Iserninus. The nationality of the other man, Auxilius, is unknown—but the Irish call him Ausaille.

At least fourteen years passed from the ordination of Patrick until the day that he set out for Ireland. The long delay cannot be accounted for simply by the necessities of an ecclesiastical training. There must have been other impediments and difficulties. He himself intimates that he was not encouraged. Those to whom he looked to for counsel considered his project rash and Patrick unqualified. His *rusticitas*, or lack of a liberal education, was marked against him; and perhaps a failure to win support is a sufficient explanation for the delay.

We can suppose that Patrick had a discreet, if not sympathetic, guide in the head of the church of Auxerre. Amator had been succeeded by one who was to bear a more illustrious name in the ecclesiastical annals of Gaul. Germanus of Auxerre is a case, common in Gaul and elsewhere during this period, of a distinguished layman who held office in the state, but then exchanged a secular for an ecclesiastical office. In 429, it devolved on him to visit Britain, and this enterprise must have had a particular interest for Patrick. The poison of the serpent Pelagius, as his opponents named him, had been spreading, in a diluted form, throughout the island. Some of the writings of Pelagius's British advocates are, in fact, still extant. The orthodox pillars of the British church were alarmed, and they sent urgent messages across the sea to invite their Gallic brethren to send able champions over to overcome the heresy. It was probably to Auxerre and Troyes, in the first instance, that they made their appeal, and it is recorded that at a synod held at Troyes it was declared that Germanus should proceed to Britain along with Lupus, bishop of Troyes, who had formally been a monk of Lerins. Whatever may be the truth about this alleged Gallic synod, Germanus certainly went with higher authority and prestige, for he traveled under the direct sanction of Celestine I, the bishop of Rome. We know that all of this transpired by the sanctioning of the deacon Palladius, who may possibly have been a deacon of Germanus. By all accounts, this authoritative mission from Gaul seems to have crushed the heretics, and their doctrine was compelled to hide its head in Britain for a few years to come.

Pope Celestine was approached soon afterwards on a subject that touched Patrick even closer than the suppression of heresy in Britain. His attention was drawn to the position of the Christian communities in Ireland. The man who interested him in this matter was the same deacon, Palladius. It is remarkable that this first appearance of Irish Christianity in ecclesiastical history should be associated, both chronologically and in the person of Palladius, with the Pelagian question. We may be fairly certain that some overture or message had come from the Christian groups in Ireland, whether to Britain or Gaul or to Rome itself, for the pope would not have sent them a bishop unless they had said that they wanted one. It is possible, then, that the motive of the Irish Christians in taking such a step at that moment may have been the same Pelagian difficulty that had caused the appeal from Britain. And if the Pelagian heresy had gained any ground in Ireland, nothing would have been more natural than that the fact should have come to the notice of Germanus while he was dealing with the same question in Britain.

This line of conjecture may offer us a way to understand a passage from Patrick's autobiographical sketch—his *Confession*. He complains of the treachery of an intimate friend whom he doesn't name, but who seems from the circumstances to have been an ecclesiastic, either of Britain or Gaul. He had communicated his inmost thoughts to this friend, and had evidently received sympathy from him regarding his plan of working in Ireland. The friend told Patrick emphatically that he must be made a bishop. And afterwards, when the question of choosing a bishop for Ireland arose, his friend actively urged on Patrick's behalf. Now, it was in Britain that the matter of a bishop was discussed. We have an incident, here, which fits exactly into the situation when Germanus was fighting against heresy in Britain in 429. If the same heresy existed in Ireland at that time, then Germanus would have had to deal with it there, as well. It seems reasonable to suggest that Germanus was that unnamed friend of Patrick in those days, and that orthodox members of the Irish communities sent representatives to Germanus while he was in Britain combating heresy, asking for some intervention in their own communities. The question of sending a bishop to guide the Irish Christians in the right path became at once practical and urgent. Patrick was the suitable man for the post.

The opportunity for which he had been waiting seemed now to have come at last. There had been interest in Irish Christianity before in Gaul, and especially at Auxerre, but it was now brought under the notice of the head of Christendom. There seemed to be prospects now for Patrick to undertake the work on which he had set his heart, under high sanction and with sufficient support. But Pope Celestine selected another. The deacon Palladius, who had been active in these affairs, was prepared to go to Ireland, and Celestine consecrated him bishop for that purpose in 431. The choice was, in fact, perfectly natural. We must remember that the first and primary consideration of the Pope was the welfare and orthodoxy of Irish believers, not the conversion of Irish unbelievers. He was called on to meet the need of the Christian communities, and the further spreading of the faith among the heathen was an ulterior consideration. Therefore, the qualification that he sought in the new bishop may not have been a burning zeal for preaching to pagans, but rather experience and capacity for dealing with the Pelagian heresy. Palladius had taken a prominent role in coping with this heresy in Britain, and it is probable that he had accompanied Germanus there. Irish Christians may have, in fact, intimated that they wished for his appointment.

Wilfrid's Example

Feelings of division between Catholic Christianity on the British Isles and Roman Catholicism elsewhere have ancient origins, long before King Henry VIII declared the Church of England separate from the Roman Church at the Protestant Reformation. St. Wilfrid's (d. 709) life is a good example of this conflict of worldviews in the first millennium, after St. Patrick. He was an Anglo-Saxon from Northumbria who was first trained by Irish monks at Lindisfarne Abbey while still a boy. *The Life of Wilfrid* tells how the Holy Ghost prompted young Wilfrid to go to Rome, "to visit the See of St. Peter, Prince of the Apostles, a road hitherto untraveled by our people, believing that he would wash away every trace of sin thereby and receive a great blessing." After leaving Lindisfarne to complete his studies in Rome, Wilfrid then returned to England and argued the Roman side at the Synod of Whitby (where the Northumbrian king decided to calculate the date of Easter according to Roman ways, rather than by more indigenous practices). Wilfrid was never very welcome as a bishop in his native land again, feeling far more "at home" in Roman Gaul (Farmer, 108).

CHAPTER SIX

Palladius and Patrick

The brief chronicle of Palladius's visit to Ireland states that he came and went within only a year. It is generally assumed that he did not have the strength, nor the tact, to deal with the situation; that he departed in despair; and that his mission was a failure. But our evidence does not warrant those conclusions. We are told that he proceeded from Ireland to the land of the Picts in north Britain, and that he died there. Tradition associates the brief episode of Palladius with the regions of north Leinster (the old kingdom of Leinster, or Laigin, south of the River Liffey) and the hills of Wicklow. We can't be sure that he did not intend to return. The most probable conclusion seems that the episcopate of Palladius in Ireland was cut short, not by a voluntary desertion of his post, but by death.

Who Came First to Ireland?

Scholars disagree, and for good reasons; there are convincing arguments that Patrick may have preceded Palladius. "If Palladius really worked in Ireland before Patrick, why does the latter, whose writings show him to have been the most generous as well as the humblest of men, pay no tribute whatever to his predecessor in the mission, more especially if . . . Palladius had suffered martyrdom at the hands of the pagan Irish?" (Binchy, 31).

We would like to know where were the dwelling places of the Christians to whom Palladius was sent. Between the port where Wicklow of the Vikings now is—the place where Palladius landed—and the lonely glen of the two lakes by whose shores a cluster of churches afterwards sprung up, stretched the lands of the children of Garrchu; tradition says that the chief of this tribe regarded Palladius with disfavor.

His short sojourn is also associated with the foundation of three churches. One of them was a little house for praying, built by him or his disciples, on a high wooded hill that rises sheer on the left bank of the River Avoca. Farther west, beyond the hills, we can determine with more certainty another place that tradition associates with the activity of Palladius, in the neighborhood of one of the royal seats of the lords of Leinster. He is said to have founded a church that was known as the *domnach*, or "Lord's house," in a hilly region that is strewn with the remnants of ancient generations. The original church of this place has long since vanished, and its precise site cannot be known with any certainty. At Donard we feel with some assurance that we are at one of the earliest homes of the Christian faith in Ireland, not the earliest that existed, but the earliest to which we can give a name. There was a third church, seemingly the most important of those that Palladius is said to have founded, called Cell Fine, "the church of the tribes," in which his tablets and certain books and relics brought from Rome were preserved. Perhaps there only, in a place unknown to us, was his memory preserved.

Whatever his qualities may have been, he was in Ireland for too short of a time to have produced a permanent impression. The historical significance of his appearance in Ireland does not rest only on whatever slight ecclesiastical or theological successes he may have accomplished. It is significant because it was the first manifestation in Ireland of the authority of Rome. The secular arm of Rome, in days when Rome was mightier, had never reached the Scottish, or Gaelic, coast; it was not until after the mother of the empire had been besieged and despoiled by barbarian invaders that her new spiritual dominion began to reach out to remoter shores where her worldly power had never sought. The coming of Palladius was the first link in the chain that bound Ireland, for some centuries very loosely, to the spiritual center of western Europe.

But when we are seeking vainly for traces of this first spiritual comer to the children of Garrchu and the holy hill of Donard, we are reminded that, if his coming is significant, it is also because no secular messengers of Rome had come before him. The superstitious and primitive customs of the island were protected and secured, pure and uncontaminated, by the barrier of sundering seas. If one of the early Roman Emperors had annexed Ireland to their British provinces, ideas of city life and civil government and administration would have been introduced that might have proved a more powerful

The Toothless Legend

Wicklow is one of those words whose native meaning is both funny and telling. In the original Irish, the name actually means "church of the toothless one." It is the name of both a county and a town, south of Dublin, on the eastern coast. Tradition says that Wicklow was founded by the Vikings, during the invasions in the late ninth century, but the "toothless one" reference comes from an earlier legend of St. Patrick. He and a group of his fellow missionaries attempted to land on the shore there, but were attacked by the locals. One of the men had his tooth dislodged, but the party still persevered and founded a church in that place.

solvent than Christianity of Celtic and Iberian barbarism. A Roman outpost might have, in a couple of hundred years, produced a greater change in civilization than all the little clerical communities that sprang up in the three or four centuries after the coming of Palladius. It would have been the task of the Roman government to put an end to the incessant petty wars between the kingdoms and tribes: *pacisque imponere morem*, "impose the habit of peace." But the absence of such civilizing influence protected and preserved the native traditions, and the curiosity of those who study the development of the human mind may be glad that Ireland lay safe and undisturbed at the end of the world, and that Palladius, nearly a hundred years after the death of Constantine, was the first emissary from Rome.

Patrick's Consecration

The appointment of Palladius as bishop for the Scots naturally affected Patrick's plans. He no longer had a motive for delay in setting out to accomplish his project. There was no reason why, with the support of Auxerre and Bishop Germanus, he couldn't set out, along with whatever cohorts he could muster, and, under the auspices of the new bishop, begin the conversion of the heathen. Everything was arranged for his enterprise in the following year, AD 432, and the tradition is that he had already set out from Auxerre, accompanied by an elderly presbyter named Segitius, when the news reached Gaul that Palladius was dead. The announcement was brought by some of the companions of Palladius, and once again Patrick's plans were interrupted. But only for a moment. The circumstances seem to imply that there was a distinct understanding that he was to be the successor to the bishop, and Germanus consecrated him immediately. Patrick heard of the death of Palladius at some place on the road from Auxerre to the channel, and his natural course was to return to Auxerre and receive ordination from his master.

The oldest evidence of Patrick's consecration—and we have no independent source to supplement it—is the account in Muirchu's *Life*. It is stated there that Patrick, learning at Ebmoria (probably somewhere between Auxerre and the north coast of Gaul) of the death of Palladius, interrupted his journey northwards and went to a certain bishop, who conferred upon him episcopal ordination. This bishop is designated *eapiscopum Amatho rege*, and is described in terms that imply he was eminent and well known. Now we know of no Gallic bishop called Amathorex, and we know of no Gallic bishop alive in the year 432 whose name at all resembles *Amatho regem*. But we do know of an eminent Gallic bishop named Amator, whose episcopal seat was at Auxerre, where Patrick received at least part of his ecclesiastical training. Only Amator died in 418, and therefore couldn't have ordained Patrick bishop in 432.

Nevertheless, there can hardly be a doubt that Amator is the one intended, for he is the only Gallic bishop of similar name in Patrick's time. When we examine closely the narrative of Muirchu we find a statement that is inconsistent with the assertion that Patrick was ordained bishop by *Amatho rege*. We are told that when he started from Auxerre for Ireland in the company of Segitius the presbyter, he had "not yet been ordained bishop by Germanus." This clearly implies that the prelate who ordained him bishop was none other than Germanus, just what we would expect. But then, where did the confusion arise for Muirchu? It is probably rather simple; the narrator confused Patrick's ordination as bishop with his ordination as deacon. This solution fits in perfectly with the interpretation of *Amatho rege* as analogous to *Amatore*. Bishop Amator, Germanus' predecessor, ordained Patrick deacon either before, or in, 418.

So it came about that, in the end, Patrick started for the field of his work invested with the authority and office that would render his labors most effective. Considerable preparation must have been made. To carry out the ambitious plans for converting heathen lands, there would have been need for not only a company of fellow workers, but a cargo of spiritual treasures and ecclesiastical gear for the equipment of the new communities that were to be founded. There is no better illustration of these "spiritual treasures" than what can be found in Pope Gregory's provisions for the mission of St. Augustine of Canterbury to England in the 590s, as recorded in Bede's *Ecclesiastical History*: "Pope Gregory, hearing from Bishop Augustine, that he had a great harvest, and but few laborers, sent to him, together with his messengers, several fellow laborers and ministers of the word of whom the first and principal were Mellitus, Justus, Paulinus, and Rufinianus, and by them all things in general that were necessary for the worship and service of the church, such as sacred vessels and vestments for the altars, also ornaments for the churches, vestments for the priests and clerks, relics of the holy apostles and martyrs, and many books" (Book I.29). Also, money and treasure were indispensable, and however

Patrick's Liturgical Objects

"Tirechan [one of the earliest biographers] notes that Patrick had brought the required liturgical items across the Shannon: bells, chalices, patens, altar stones, books of the law and gospel books. None of these is described as luxurious or decorated. This stands in sharp contrast to Aldhelm's contemporary description of the very luxurious vessels used at Bugga's church in Anglo-Saxon England, to Wilfrid's use of gold and purple silk hangings in his church at Ripon, and to Cogitosus's description of the lavishly decorated church of St. Brigid in Kildare. Thus Patrick's mission is credited with an austerity coinciding with earlier Pelagian ideals, perhaps reflecting a consciousness of the earlier, more austere attitude" (Herren/Brown, 190).

simple Patrick's faith may have been in the intrinsic potency of the gospel that he was inspired to preach, he was a man of thoroughly practical mind. And he knew that silver and gold and worldly wealth would be needed in dealing with pagan princes, and in the effective establishment of clerical communities.

The following account of Patrick's setting out for the field of his laborers is based on a critical examination of the oldest sources. In recent days, scholars have wished to believe that he too, like Palladius, was consecrated by Pope Celestine. Such a consecration seemed to both add a halo of dignity to the national saint and to link his church more closely to the apostolic seat. We have no means of knowing whether Patrick set out before or after the death of Pope Celestine, but in any case the pious story is inconsistent with the oldest testimonies. Even so, the point has very little theoretical or practical importance. By virtue of what had already happened, Ireland was in principle as closely linked to Rome as any western church. The circumstances of the consecration and mission of Palladius were significant; but whether his successor was ordained at Rome or at Auxerre, whether he was personally known to the Roman pontiff or not, was a matter of little notice.

The position of the Roman see at this period in the Western Church is often only vaguely understood. At the end of the fourth century the bishops of Rome, beyond their acknowledged primacy in Christendom, possessed at least two important rights that secured them a large influence in the ecclesiastical affairs of the western provinces of the empire. The bishop of Rome was recognized by imperial decrees of Emperors Valentinian I (d. 375) and Gratian (d. 383) as a court to which clergy might appeal from the decisions of provincial councils in any part of the western portion of the empire. Equally important, although unrecognized by any formal decree, the Roman church was also regarded as the model church, and when doubtful points of discipline arose, the bishops of the Gallic or other provinces used to consult the bishop of Rome for guidance. The answers of the Roman bishops to such questions are called decretals. No decretals are preserved older than those of Pope Damasus I (d. 384), and perhaps it was during his pontificate that the practice of making these applications became common. The motive of the custom is clear; it was to preserve uniformity of discipline throughout the church and prevent the growth of divergent practices. But those who consulted the Roman pontiff were not in any way bound to accept his ruling. The decretal was an answer to a question, rather than a command. Those who accepted it were merely imitating the Roman see, not obeying it.

Bishop Patrick

Bury discounts the importance of where Patrick was ordained a bishop, but this hasn't kept scholars from debating the point ever since. One of the most prominent scholars argues for Britain instead of Gaul as the place of consecration, and disregards the notion that the bishop of Rome would have been directly involved: "Patrick must have been consecrated in Britain, either by three bishops if the practice of the Western Church as a whole was followed, or by a single bishop if the contrary Celtic practice was already in existence" (Binchy, 32).

In the latter part of the fourth century, the nascent authority of the Roman bishop was confronted by a serious rival. When Milan, rather than Rome, became the imperial residence in Italy, the see of Milan assumed immediately a new importance and prestige. Its bishop soon came to be regarded as an authority to whom appeals might be addressed, as well as to the bishop of Rome. This new dignity was further justified by the exemplary personality of Ambrose (d. 397), who then occupied the see. If he had remained longer in that capacity, it is possible that Milan would have become to Rome what Constantinople became—because it was an imperial city—in regard to Alexandria and Antioch.

When a new ecclesiastical province was to be added to western Christendom, it was to Rome, the "apostolic seat," that an appeal would be made. The bishop of Rome represented the unity of the church, and the Christians of Ireland, desiring to be an organized portion of that unity, would naturally look to him to speed them on their way. His recognition of Ireland as a province of the spiritual federation would be the most direct and effective means of securing for it an established place among the western churches. If then, they had asked Pope Celestine to either choose a bishop for them, or confirm their own choice and consecrate a bishop of their choosing, they adopted exactly the course that we might expect. But once this step was taken, once the Roman bishop had given his sanction, it was a matter of indifference who actually consecrated his successor. The essential point is that by the sending of Palladius, Ireland had become one of the western churches, and therefore, looked to the see of Rome as the highest authority in Christendom.

CHAPTER SEVEN

Political and Social Conditions at That Time

Irish society remained in the primitive stage of tribal organization for more than a thousand years after the island first became part of Christendom. The land was divided into a large number of small districts, each of which was owned by a *Tuath*, a common people, or tribe. At the head of the tribe was a "king" who was elected from a certain family. Below the king were four social grades within the tribe. There were the nobles, who were distinguished by the possession of land. After these fortunate ones came those who had wealth in cattle and other movable property but were only tenants of the land on which they lived. Below these were those people who owned no property or cattle, but farmed lands by paying rent. At the lowest rung on the social ladder were two categories of slaves; the first were laborers of all kinds who were still members of the tribe, deserving of its protection; and the other class of slaves did not belong to the tribe, and were instead strangers, such as fugitives and captives. Patrick belonged to this class, *fudirs* as they were called, in his earlier days of bondage.

The range of these small tribal kingdoms can still be approximately traced, for they are represented, in large part, by the baronies of the modern map of Ireland. And the names of the baronies in many cases preserve the names of the tribes. By inspecting a map on which the baronies are marked, you will receive a general idea of the number and size of the small kingdoms which formed the political units of the island. They varied greatly in size, as well as in numbers and importance. But each kingdom, whether large or small, managed its own affairs. The self-government of the tribes and the complicated organization of the clans and families within them were the most important and fundamental social facts of life in Ireland in late antiquity.

Ireland was then organized in an ascending scale of kings and over-kings. There was the high-king at the head of all. Below him were six over-kings: Cashel, Connaught, Laigin, Aileach, Ulaid, and Oriel. Below these were the tribal kings, who were overlords of several small territories. For example, several of the small kingdoms in north Munster formed an intermediate group, the kingdom of Thomond. It is clear that this system grew up by degrees through conquest, and one remarkable practice illustrates the point. It was the habit of the over-kings to take hostages from the under-kings, as a surety for the fulfillment of their obligations. This was such an important feature of the political system that a house for the custody of hostages was an almost indispensable addition to a royal palace. The "mound of the hostages" is still something to be seen at the mystical Hill of Tara. The ceaseless warfare that marks the annals of Ireland suggests that these bonds were as much a cause of trouble as they were a source of union.

We know practically nothing about the political relations that existed in Ireland in the fifth century. The most important fact seems to be that the descendants of King Eochaid (d. 366), and particularly the family of his son Niall (d. 405), both high-kings, were winning power in the northern half of the island. When Patrick came, Laoghaire (d. 463), a son of Niall, was on the throne of Tara, and his cousin was king of Connaught. As we will see, Laoghaire's reign seems to have been a relatively peaceful period, if such an epithet may be applied to any epoch of Irish history. Whatever may have been the measure of the high-king's authority, it was unquestionably desirable for the new bishop, in pursuing his plans, to secure his favor or neutrality.

But the real prospect of success for Patrick depended mainly on gaining the favor or neutrality of the tribal kings and the heads of families. The king of Ulidia might tolerate or encourage the new, strange worship in his immediate territory, or embrace the faith for himself, or simply recommend it; but although his example might have a great influence, he couldn't force any under-king and his tribe to tolerate the presence of a Christian community within their borders.

Patrick came to Ireland not only to make individual converts, but to build up a society of priests. A church and a priesthood must have

St. Patrick and King Arthur of the Round Table

The moniker, high-king, does not only appear in the annals of Irish history. The priestly writer Geoffrey of Monmouth, early chronicler of King Arthur and the Knights of the Round Table legends, wrote in about AD 1150 of Arthur as the high-king of Britain. There are actually many Arthurs of Scottish, Welsh, Irish, and Anglo-Saxon history at this time, from the early fifth century on. Some legends talk of Arthur as the grandson of the emperor Constantine. In Geoffrey of Monmouth's account, Arthur assumes the throne at the age of fifteen, after the death of his father. Arthur then moves from battle to battle, conquering the Scots, Picts, all of Ireland, and most of present-day Scandinavia, as well as Gaul, uniting them all under one wide-reaching throne for Britain. Very few scholars today would accept these details, and most, in fact, believe that the King Arthur of legend never actually existed. But the legends would have that this all happened about one hundred years after the time of Patrick.

means of support, and in a country where wealth consisted in land and cattle it was clear that, if the church was to become a stable and powerful institution, its priests and ministers must have lands secured for their use. But land could only be obtained through the goodwill of those who possessed it; therefore, it was impossible to plant a church in any territory until some noble who owned a private estate had been persuaded to accept Christian baptism and make a grant of land for ecclesiastical use—with his tribe's consent. The conversion of the landless classes, slaves, farmers, and even the lords of herds, couldn't lead to the foundation of churches and the maintenance of sacerdotal institutions. Patrick's success depended on the kings of the tribes and the chiefs of the clans.

There was another reason why Christianity couldn't hope to make considerable progress until the heads of society had been converted. Strong tribal sentiment, expressed in the devotion of tribesmen to their king and clansmen to their chief, was the most powerful social bond. And while, if a chief accepted the new faith his clan would generally follow his example, it was unlikely that if he rejected it many of his followers would dissociate themselves from his action. On every account the process of establishing the Christian worship and priesthood in Ireland must begin from above and not from below.

Cults, the Druids, and Sorcery

We know little of the religious beliefs and cults in Ireland that were eventually displaced by Christian faith. If there was any one divinity that was revered and worshiped throughout the land it was probably the sun. There seem to have been no temples, but there were altars in the open air, and idols were worshiped, especially in the form of pillar-stones. Various gods and goddesses play a part in the tales of Irish mythology, but it is unknown whether any of these beings was honored by a cult. There was no priesthood, and it seems certain that there was no organized religion that could be described as national.

Heathen ways were no opposition compared to the weapons of such a force as the organized religion that had swept the Roman Empire. Heathenism is naturally tolerant, and when there is no powerful priestly order jealous of its privileges and monopoly, a new superstition is entertained readily. We should probably admit that the morality enjoined by the Christian faith, and the hopes that such faith offers, would have hardly appealed to heathen peoples or taken possession of their minds if it had not first engaged their imaginations by mysteries and rites. Above all, it was these mysterious rites—baptism, and the mystical ceremony that is known as the Eucharist—that stamped the religion as genuine in the eyes of barbarians. While Christianity demanded that its converts abandon heathen observances and heathen cults, it didn't require them to surrender their belief in the existence of the beings whom they were forbidden to worship. They were only required to regard those beings in a new light, as maleficent demons.

Early Christians in Ireland, even the highest authorities in the church, were as superstitious as the heathen. The belief in the *sidhe*, or fairies, was universal in Ireland and was not affected by Christianity. These beliefs often survive even today. And so the spreading of the new religion was facilitated by the willingness to allow heathen superstitions and intellectual absurdities to remain, aiming at transcending and transforming them instead, so that fear of deities could be turned into a hatred of demons.

The primary pretenders to the possession of wizardry and powers of divinization in Ireland were the Druids. They combined supernatural lore with innocent secular learning, skill in poetry, and knowledge of the laws and history of their country. They gave the kings advice and educated their children. The high value attached to their counsels also rested naturally on their prophetic powers. They practiced divination in various forms, with inscribed rods of yew, for instance, or by means of magic wheels. They could raise the winds, cover the plains with darkness, create envelopes of vapor that rendered those that moved in them invisible. Although they were learned in divine things, they didn't form a priestly class, and in their religious functions they might instead be compared to augurs than to priests. It was their habit to shave their heads in front from ear to ear and to wear white garments. They were unfriendly to the introduction of new beliefs that might threaten their own position, since it condemned the practice of divination and those kindred arts that were the basis for their eminent power. But their opposition was ineffective because they had no organization.

It became an advantage for the Christian church to recognize demons as an actual power that stood on the same intellectual plane as the heathen. The belief in demons as a foe with which the church had to deal was expressed officially in the institution of a clerical order called exorcists, whose duty it became to exorcize devils at baptism. Patrick had exorcists in his company, and it was important that the Christian, going forth to persuade the heathen, had such equipments of superstition. He was able to meet the heathen sorcerer on common ground because he believed in the sorceries that he condemned. In the remarkable ancient Irish Christian incantation, the Lorica of St. Patrick, the Trinity, angels, prophets, and other Christian powers are invoked, but also "might of heaven, brightness of sun, brilliance of moon, splendor of fire, speed of light, swiftness of wind, depth of sea, stability of earth, firmness of rock," to intervene between he who repeats the spell when he rises in the morning and "every fierce merciless force that may come upon my body and soul, against incantations of false prophets, against black laws of paganism, against false laws of heresy, against deceit of idolatry, against spells of women and smiths and Druids, against all knowledge that is forbidden the human soul."

Student Patrick

Patrick was not a scholar himself, although he clearly knew the Bible and a little Latin. But it is possible that more learned Christians than Patrick lived in Ireland before he arrived; they may have fled Britain and Gaul in advance of the barbarian invasions that plagued both areas in those centuries. In his *Confession*, Patrick includes this line: "Therefore be amazed, both great and small who fear God; rhetoricians and you of the Lord," which has led some to think that he was addressing scholars of some sort. However, it is more likely that he was addressing the Druids.

Patrick was as fully convinced as the pagan that the powers of magicians were real, but he knew that those powers were strictly limited, while the power of his own God was limitless. Patrick could never have said to an Irish wizard, as children of the Enlightenment would now say, "Your magic is an imposture; your spells cannot really raise spirits or control the forces of nature; you cannot foretell what is to come." He would have said, "Yes, you can do such miracles by the aid of evil powers, but those powers are subject to a good power whose religion I preach, and are impotent except through his permission." This point of intellectual agreement between the pre-Enlightenment

Christian priest and the heathen, their common acceptance of the efficacy of sorcery, even though they put different interpretations on its conditions, was probably a significant aid in the propagation of the Christian religion. If Christianity had offered to people only its new theological doctrine with the hope of eternal life and its new ethical ideals; if it had come simple and unadorned without an armory of mysteries, miracles, and rites; if it had risen to the height of rejecting magic not because it was wicked but because it was absurd—it could never have won half the world.

The spread of new religious ideas naturally excited the misgivings of the Druids, unless they were to be professed only here and there in isolated households. Shortly before the coming of Palladius, they probably awoke to the fact that a faith opposed to their own interests was gaining ground. At the same time, the Christian communities were discovering that they deserved and required a bishop and an ecclesiastical organization. These Druidic apprehensions may be reflected in a prophecy attributed to the wizards of the high-king. They foretold that a foreign doctrine would seduce the people, overthrow kings, and subvert the old order of things, and they designated the preacher of the doctrine in these oracular words: "Adze-head will come with a crook-head staff; in his house, with hold-head robe, he will chant impiety from his table; from the front part of his house all his household will respond, 'So be it, so be it.'"

It would be illegitimate to build any theory on an alleged prophecy, when we cannot determine its date. But we may admit without hesitation that this ancient verse composed by a pagan fairly represents the tradition that was current before the coming of Patrick. The knowledge that it demonstrates of Christian language, as Christianity was already somewhat known and had already won converts in Ireland, shows what the Druids understood before the coming of Palladius's successor. In fact, the Druids may have known that the Christians of Ireland, such as they were, had requested the appointment of a bishop a year or two before the sending of Palladius. The Druids have then expressed their apprehensions in the form of this oracle. But whether the oracle circulated in the mouths of people before the appearance of Palladius and Patrick, or was first declared at a later time, it possesses historical significance as reflecting the agitation of heathenism, roused to alarm at the growth of a new and foreign worship.

Druid Magi

"Something is also to be learnt from the use made of the Celtic words for Druid in the Celtic literatures of later times. Among the oldest instances in Welsh poetry of the use of the word *derwyddon*, Druids, is one where it is applied to the Magi or Wise Men, who came with presents to the infant Jesus, and its Irish cognate *drui* is not only used in the same manner, but is usually rendered into Latin by *magus*, a magician. . . . [There is also] the fervent writer of an ancient hymn ascribed to St. Columba, who is therein made to say: Christ the son of God is my Druid" (Rhys, 69–71).

CHAPTER EIGHT

The First Mission

The spot where the River Vartry, once the Dee, reaches the coast, just north of the long ness that runs out into the sea at Wicklow, has a historical interest for the study of St. Patrick. This little river mouth was a chief port for mariners of the island in ancient times coming from both south Britain and Gaul, a place where strangers and traders landed and where the natives often caught sight of outlandish ships and foreign faces. It was the port where Patrick would most naturally land coming from south Britain. But in any case, he could hardly do otherwise than first seek the region where Palladius had labored briefly. This would be the natural starting point, the place for studying the situation, forming plans, perhaps for the opening

Two Separate Missions?

One of the most influential Patriciologists (those who study Patrick) has argued that there were two separate missions going on in Ireland in the fifth century: Patrick's, and the work of those who were left by Palladius. "The surviving members of the first mission were still functioning independently in other areas, and even the physical difficulties of communicating with them must have been very formidable. When one remembers that fifth-century Ireland contained well over a hundred separate tribal kingdoms, many of which were constantly hostile to their neighbours, one realizes how hazardous an undertaking it was for a stranger to pass even from one tribe to another. . . . [T]he existence over a certain period of two missions side by side, an earlier one commissioned by the Papacy and staffed by a few Continental bishops, and a later one organized in Britain, which worked in the hitherto unevangelised North, seems to be the least improbable solution. . . . Whether both were eventually amalgamated under the leadership of Patrick or whether this fusion has been artificially created by the spread of the Patrick legend we shall probably never know" (Binchy, 148).

of negotiations. There is no definitive record of this first stage in the new bishop's work, and our ignorance of his relations to these communities in southern Ireland is one of the most unfortunate gaps in our meager knowledge of his life. No sooner has he landed in the kingdom of Leinster than tradition transports him to the kingdom of Ulidia.

We must see where this tradition—this Ulidian tradition—would lead, although we cannot allow it to guide us blindly. There are two connected narratives that purport to describe important passages of Patrick's early work in Ireland. One of these, the memoir by Tirechan, contains some genuine and unvarnished records as to Christian communities that he founded. The other, the *Life of St. Patrick* by Muirchu, is full of stories that are difficult to utilize for historical purposes, although it must be admitted that they have elements of historical value. The most striking parts of Muirchu's account are pure legend, but they are framed in a setting that might include some literal facts. And the historical background is there, although we have to allow for some distortion by anti-pagan motives. It is difficult for the critic to find a clear way in dealing with this mixed material. Most of those who have undertaken the task have adopted a crude and vain method of retaining as historical what is not miraculous. There is much that we can securely reject at once, but there are other things that, while we are not at liberty to accept them, we must regard as possibly resting on some authentic basis. We don't have the data for a definite solution. It seems best, then, to reproduce the story, to critique it, and to point out what may be its implications.

If we stand on the steep headland that towers above the sea halfway between the towns of Wicklow and Dublin, the eye reaches from the long low hill prominence under which the southern town is built, northward to the island of Lambay. A little beyond, hidden from the view and close to the coast, are some small islets that in ancient days were known as the isles of the Children of Cor. If we could see these minute points of land we would be able to take in, with a sweep of the eye, the first stage of St. Patrick's traditional journey as he steered his boat northward from the mouth of the Dee to bear his message to the people of Ulidia. The story tells that he landed on one of these islets, ever since, it has been known as Inis Patrick. The name attests to the association with the apostle. If he traveled to Ulidia by sea, it would have been a natural precaution, in days when travelers might be suspected as outlaws or robbers, to land for a night's stop on a desert island rather than on the coast, where meaner inhabitants might give a stranger a more unpleasant welcome. From the island that bears his name he continued his course along the coast of Meath, past the mouth of the River Boyne, and along the shores of Conaille Muirthemne, which formed the southern part of the Ulidian kingdom. This was the country where in old days Setanta, the lord of the march, is said to have kept watch and ward over the gates of Ulster. But it was more northern parts of the Pictish kingdom that Patrick intended to reach, and he steered on past the inlet that was not yet the fiord of the Carlings, past the mountainous region of southern Dalaradia, until he came at last to a little landlocked bay.

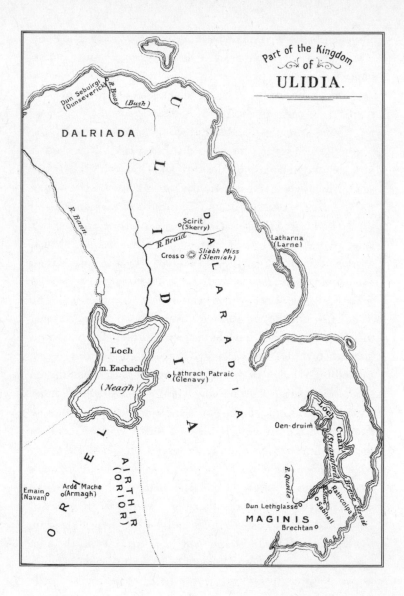

Part of the Kingdom
of
ULIDIA.

DALRIADA

U L I D I A

Dun Seburg
(Dunseverick)   R. Bus   (Bush)

R. Bann

R. Braid

Scirit
(Skerry)

Cross o   Sliabh Miss
(Slemish)

Latharna
(Larne)

D A L A R A D I A

Loch
n. Eachach
(Neagh)

Lathrach Patraic
(Glenavy)

Oen-druim

Loch Cuan
(Strangford)

Brene Strait

O R I E L

AIRTHIR
(ORIOR)

Emain
(Navan)

Ardd Mache
(Armagh)

R. Quoile

Dun Lethglasse

Rathcolpa

Saahall

MAGINIS

Brechtan

The sea portal to Strangford Lough, as it is now called, is a narrow strait. Patrick rowed into this water and landed on the southern shore of the bay at the mouth of the Slan stream, which until recent years was known by its old name. They hid their boat, we are told, and went a short distance inward from the shore to find a place of rest. Had they rowed farther westward and followed the banks of the winding River Quoile, they would have soon come to a great fortress, Dun Lethglasse. A swineherd espied the strangers from his hut, and supposing them to be thieves and robbers, went out and told his master. The region is embossed with small hills, and one of the higher of these hills was the master's abode. Dichu was the man's name who announced their arrival, and he was one of those "naturally good" men whom Patrick, though he was not a Pelagian, may have been prepared to find among pagan folk. At the tidings of his herd, Dichu was prepared to slay the strangers, but when he looked upon the face of Patrick he changed his mind and offered hospitality. Then Patrick taught him and the man believed, becoming the first convert won by the apostle in the land of the Scots.

Before we ask the questions that naturally arise when we hear a tale such as this, we must first accompany the saint on another stage in his progress. He tarried with Dichu for only a few days, for he was impatient to carry out a purpose that he cherished of revisiting the scene of his thralldom and the home of his old master, Miliucc, in the extreme north of Dalaradia. He left his boat in the keeping of Dichu and journeyed by

> **Sacred Rivers**
>
> "Every locality had its divinity, and the rivers were specially identified with certain divine beings, as witness the streams that still bear the name of Dee and kindred ones" (Rhys, 67–68).

land through the country of the Picts until he saw once more the slopes of Mount Miss. Miliucc was still alive, and Patrick wished to pay the master from whom he had fled the price of his freedom. It is not supposed that he deemed it necessary to visit, as if to make legal his liberty and secure himself against the claim of a master to seize a fugitive slave. Instead, it seems that he hoped to convert Miliucc to the Christian faith. But the heathen chief, hearing that he was approaching with this intent, and seized with a strange alarm lest his former slave should by some irresistible spell constrain him to embrace a new religion against his will, resorted to an extreme device. Gathering all of his goods together into his wooden house, he set fire to the building, and perished inside of it. The flames of the unexpected pyre met Patrick's eyes as he stood on the southwestern side of Mount Miss, and his biographer pictures him standing for two or three hours dumb with surprise and grief. "I do not know, God knows," he said, using a favorite phrase, "whether the posterity of this man will not serve others forever, and no king arise from his seed." Then he turned back and retraced his steps to the habitation of Dichu. A cross, mentioned by Muirchu, was erected on the spot where the legend supposed Patrick to have stood, and the memory of this is still preserved in the name of the townland of Cross, on a hill to the west of Slemish.

The funeral pyre of Mount Miss sends our thoughts over sea and land to a more famous pyre at Sardis, in the ancient kingdom of Lydia. The self-immolation of the obscure Dalaradian king belongs to the same cycle of lore as that of the great Lydian monarch whose name became a proverb for luxury and wealth. Croesus (595–ca. 546 BC) built a timber death pile in the court of his palace to escape the shame of servitude to an earthly conqueror; Miliucc sought the flames to avoid the peril of thralldom under a ghostly master. But in both cases the idea of a king dying solemnly by fire is taken from some old religious usage and introduced by legendary fancy into a historical situation. And in this case, fancy has done well and ably. The desperate pyre of Patrick's former master is a pathetic symbol of the protest of a doomed religion.

The island plain of Dalaradia and the districts around Dun Lethglasse claimed to have been the part of Ireland where Patrick began his work of preaching and baptizing. He lived there and his religion grew. In later days,

Plotting the Work

One of the most recent biographers of St. Patrick agrees with Bury that the saint is not given enough credit for his organizational skills and planning in the old legends. "In reality, Patrick's mission probably succeeded because of a slow and steady approach with a careful eye to the practical politics of Irish society. More than anything else, he needed cooperation from the kings of northern Ireland if he was to minister to the Christians already there and preach the gospel to possible converts. We know from his letters that Patrick made payments to the local kings in order to gain their favor and protection" (Freeman, 90).

when the memory of Patrick had been glorified, the inhabitants of those places pleased themselves with the thought that he "chose out and loved" Dalaradia. With the help of Dichu, he established himself securely there. Dichu was clearly a chieftain of influence and authority in that region; he granted Patrick a site for a Christian establishment on a hill not far from the fortress, and a wooden barn was said to have been turned into a place of Christian worship. The rustic association has been preserved in the name that has remained ever since: Sabhall or Saul, a word that was probably borrowed from the Latin *stabulum* for cattle stall or sheepfold.

But we shouldn't suppose that the history of St. Patrick's first plunge into missionary work was so simple, or so fully left to the play of chance, as some of the early, naïve tales, represent. They belong to a class of tales that are characteristic of history in its uncritical stage—tales that invert the perspective and magnify a subordinate incident to the primary motive and purpose of the actors, ignoring the true motive or depressing it to the level of an accident. Such tales are often accepted as literally true if they hang together superficially and if the particular incidents are natural or even possible. But when you take a deeper and more critical look, they appear incredible.

The epic simplicity of Patrick's journey may be true to outward circumstances, but it is not possible to believe that he went out so purely at a venture, like one in a romance who sets forth on a quest and with a purpose, but yet content to leave his course to be guided by chance, without any previous plan or calculation. The sole motive of Patrick's northern journey is represented in some of the old tales as the hope of persuading his old master to become a Christian, where its actual and important result—the missionary work in southern Ulidia—appears almost as if it was an accidental consequence. The hard historic fact that underlies the story is the work of Patrick in Ulidia and the foundation of Saul. Recognizing this, we are unable to trust the story even so far as to trust that Ulidia was the first scene of Patrick's missionary activity. We can neither affirm this nor deny it, but we must observe that, according to another tradition with just as much authority, he began his work in the kingdom of Meath.

There is one point in the story of Miliucc, Mount Miss, and Dichu that can be accepted without question, and that is, that Dichu was certainly a real person. He was the son of Trechim, and his brother Rus was a man of influence who lived at Brechtan, which is today called Bright, a few miles south of Saul. But was this region really so completely unprepared for the reception of Christianity, as the legend supposes? Was the Christian idea a new revelation to the chieftains of Dalaradia, borne for the first time by Patrick to these northern Irish shores? It seems far more likely that there were some Christian communities already there, and that the land was ripe for conversion. In fact, some have pointed out the probability that Palladius died in this land of the Picts. If this is so—but we are treading on ground where certainty is unattainable—we might have

Britain vs. Ireland

British scholars like to emphasize that Irish Christianity owes itself in large part to Britons. But here is one of the most balanced perspectives: "The Irish Church was the creation of the British Church but after the Saxon conquest they followed different paths. British churchmen became scholars and missionaries, and Ireland became the most cultivated land in western Europe. The Irish gradually assumed the lead in Celtic religion. St. Columba, with twelve disciples, founded the monastery on the island of Iona in about 563. He converted the Picts in important parts of northern Scotland and established monasteries there. The house at Iona was the mother house and its abbots were the chief ecclesiastical rulers, superior even to bishops" (Ashe, note to illustration 144).

fresh reason to accept the claim that, when Patrick left Leinster, his first destination was Ulidia. For it would be the duty of the new bishop of the Christians in Ireland to visit and confirm the Christian communities that already existed. Other churches in the neighborhood of Saul claimed to have been planted by Patrick as well: one at Brechtan, the place of Dichu's brother, and another at Rathcolpa, that is today called Raholp.

Another, more curious, piece of evidence for the deep impression that Patrick made on the island plain of Dalaradia is the way in which the people there came to explain one of the natural features of their land in light of the miraculous powers of their teacher. According to one story, an uncivil and jealous neighbor seized two oxen of St. Patrick that were out at pasture. The saint cursed him, saying: *"Mudebrod!* You have done me wrong. Your land will never give you profit." And on the same day, the sea rushed in and covered it, and the fruitful soil was changed into a salt marsh. Another tale tells it that Patrick was resting near Druimbo, close to a salt marsh, and he heard the noise of Druids who were busily engaged in making a clay pot. It was a Sunday, and Patrick commanded them to cease their work. When they refused, he cursed them, *"Mudebrod!* May your work never profit you!" And the sea rushed in, as in the first story, and the work was destroyed.

Cursing with the Druids

Curses are common in the speech and writings of Irish saints. It was said of one popular medieval Irish saint, Ruadan, that he "loved cursing." As one contemporary writer explains it, "Early medieval Ireland was clamorous with voices blessing, praying, chanting, poetizing, satirizing, tale-telling, negotiating, murmuring, chattering, gossiping, slandering, insulting, and cursing. . . . Irish Christians who heard a biblical curse, or heard tell of a curse imitative of Christ's curses, were conscious of a turbulent Celtic past and a tribal politics based on talking—threat, prophecy, negotiation, and alliance by oath—and on violence. The Irish were specially prepared to hear saintly curses" (Bitel, 123–125). But there is much more to Irish saintly cursing than that; apparently, the Druids loved to curse; there was an old Druidic practice called "cursing from a height," where one would go to an outcrop of

We unfortunately have no idea what the curse *mudebrod* means, but the motive for these tales is probably to use the legend of the great saint's appearance in their territory to explain the origin of the salt marshes that mark the northern border of it, on the shores of Strangford Lough.

land or an overlooking tower and shout curses down upon someone passing by, allowing them to fall with great weight upon the intended recipient. And so, saints like Ruadan, who founded a monastery at Tipperary, must have occasionally found themselves in a cursing contest with the Druids.

CHAPTER NINE

Legends of Patrick and the Druids

Life in Meath, and the High-King Laoghaire

As we have already pointed out, the influence of Rome extended beyond the typical boundaries of the empire. The existence of the majestic empire was a fact never forgotten by its free neighbors; they were forced into relationship, whether hostile or peaceful, with the Roman republic. This must have affected the people of Ireland, who were the neighbors of the British and Gallic provinces of Rome, even though they were severed by narrow seas. The soil of Ireland had surely never been trodden by Roman soldiers, but its ports were not sealed to the outer world, and from the first century onward the outer world practically meant the Roman world. The people of Ireland in the fourth century must have conceived their island as lying just outside the threshold. When the grasp of Rome relaxed or her power grew weak in the neighboring provinces of Britain, the Irish would become quickly aware.

The primary channel for Roman influence around the world at this time was the infiltration of the Christian religion. The adoption of this religion by the imperial government in the fourth century must have had, as we have seen, a sensible effect in conferring prestige on Christianity beyond the boundaries of the empire. It became inevitable that the favored creed would from then on become closely associated with the empire in the minds of barbarians. For this reason, that religion acquired, on at least political grounds, a higher claim on their attention.

We must realize the force of these general considerations in order to understand the policy of the high-king who sat on the throne of Ireland throughout the whole period of Patrick's work in the island. Laoghaire had succeeded to the throne about five years before Patrick's arrival (AD 428). He was the son of King Niall, who had been slain in Britain, perhaps in the very year in which Patrick had been carried into captivity. Niall's immediate successor was his nephew, Dathi, who reigned for twenty-three years; he likewise died away from home, struck by lightning while leading a host of soldiers to drive back the Franks from the frontiers of eastern Gaul.

The reign of Laoghaire lasted thirty-six years, and it marks a new epoch in Irish history. The part that Laoghaire himself played in bringing about the changes has been underrated up until now. His statesmanship has been obscured by tradition, but it is revealed when we examine the scanty evidence.

However, it remains for us to determine the overall power and authority of the high-kings of Ireland in the under-kingdoms. It seems probable that Laoghaire exercised a lot of influence particularly in northern Ireland, as his grandfather, Eochaid, and his father, Niall, had done before him. His cousin, Amolngaid, was king of Connaught and his brothers and half-brothers were smaller kings. Whatever his real authority was, he seems to have used it in the interests of peace. So far as we can judge from the evidence of the annals, his reign was peaceful. However, he was indeed the perpetual enemy of the king of Leinster, and on three occasions at least there was war between them. On the first, Laoghaire was victorious; on the second, he was taken prisoner; and on the third, he was slain. But apart from this fatal feud we do not hear of wars and we do not hear that he went on expeditions over sea or took advantage of the difficulties of Britain, engaged

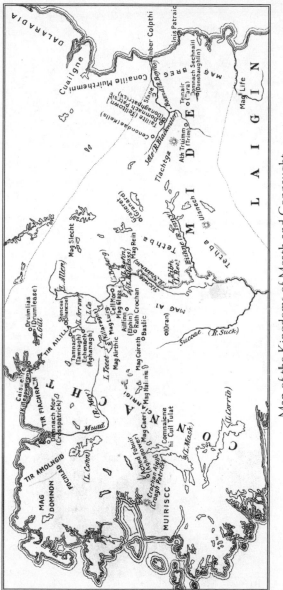

Map of the Kingdoms of Meath and Connaught

The Book of Kells

County Meath is remembered today for the monastery made famous by its most precious object. The abbey at Kells in County Meath is located about forty miles northwest of Dublin, and the famous Book of Kells was preserved there at least as early as the opening years of the ninth century AD, and perhaps earlier. It may have been written and illuminated entirely at the abbey, but there are other theories that work was begun at the more famous abbey in Iona and later transferred to Kells, where it was completed. This famous book is one of Ireland's most treasured objects, recognized around the world as one of the finest medieval illuminated manuscripts. Its contents are the four New Testament gospels, illuminated— or surrounded by small paintings and illustrations—in ways that are distinctive of the same sort of work that was being done on the continent at that time: the look of the script is bolder; the faces and hair of the evangelists distinctively northern; and other decorations, such as a warrior and what have

then in her struggle with the Saxon invaders who were to eventually conquer her.

The great question that Laoghaire had to deal with was the spread of Christianity in his dominion—a question that confronted barbarian kings just as it confronted Roman emperors, and might be as embarrassing and critical for Laoghaire in his small sphere as it had been for the ecumenical statesmen Diocletian and Constantine (Roman emperors from AD 284–305, and AD 306–337, respectively). It is clear that in the days of Emperor Theodosius II, the moment had come when the high-king of Ireland had to adopt a different attitude. If this religion was tolerated only in the south of Ireland, in the realms of Leinster and Munster, then the high-king might ignore it. But once it began to spread to his own immediate kingdom of Meath, as king of Meath he couldn't ignore it any longer. The time had come when he had to decide whether he would oppose or recognize Christian communities and priests.

come to be recognized as Celtic crosses, adorn its pages. The Book of Kells is housed today in the library of Trinity College, Dublin.

For most kings, this question would amount to: Will I myself adopt this new faith? It shows Laoghaire's exceptional ability and objectivity of vision that he was capable of separating his own personal view from his kingly policies. He was not drawn himself to the creed of Christ. He, in fact, held fast to the pagan faith and customs of his fathers, but this didn't stop him from recognizing the great and growing strength of the religion that had overflowed from the empire into his island. He saw that it had already taken root, and we may be certain that its close identification with the great empire, the union of Christ with Caesar, made for a convincing case.

It must have been difficult for the high-king to withstand the influence of the Druids on this question. They would naturally have put forth all of their effort to check the advance of the dangerous doctrine that had come from overseas to destroy their profession, their religion, and their gods. Tradition records their prophecies that the new faith, if it were to be admitted, would subvert kings and kingdoms. According to some legends, as we will see, Laoghaire appears to follow the counsels of his Druids, resolving to kill Patrick, and then yields only when the sorcery of the Christian proves stronger than that of the heathen magicians. This tale may reflect facts insofar as Laoghaire may have been inclined to persecute before he adopted his policy of evenhanded toleration. But we must not discount the possibility that—as in the case of the Frankish Clovis (d. 511) and the English Ethelbert of Kent (d. 616), there may have been friends

The Story of Ethelbert and Bertha

Ethelbert was the first king of Britain to convert to Christianity, and this seems to have come about by a combination of factors. One of them was the coming of the missionary Augustine (not to be confused with St. Augustine of Hippo) to Kent in 597; and another was his marriage to Bertha, the daughter of Charibert, the king of the Franks. The Frankish kingdom was a full member of the Roman Empire, and had been Christian for some time. In fact, most scholars assume that it was the presence of Bertha, and her influence over her husband, that allowed Pope Gregory I to send Augustine on his journey in the first place. One of Ethelbert's first acts as a Christian king cooperating with the emissary from Rome was to offer a patch of land in Canterbury, not far from the shore where Augustine had originally landed from across the channel, where a church might be built. Canterbury was also the primary seat of Ethelbert's government. The great and Gothic Canterbury Cathedral sits on this spot, now, where Augustine was of the new faith in the king's own household.

Ethelbert, too, began with the resolve to remain true to his own gods, while he granted license to the priests of his wife's faith to do their will in his realm. But before two years had passed under this arrangement, the English king was initiated in the Christian rites, while our Irish king never abandoned the faith of his fathers. Ethelbert's wife, like Clovis's, was a Christian, while of Laoghaire's we cannot say what gods she worshiped. We only have the record that she was a native of Britain, and for all we know, she may have been dead by the time Patrick arrived on the scene. And yet the fact that he had a British wife may explain some of the easy relationship between the Irish high-king and the empire, as well as Laoghaire's tolerant attitude to the Roman religion.

In the middle of the land of Meath, on the banks of the

River Boyne, a small Christian settlement arose. The place was called the "ford of the alder," and the name of the tree, Trim, is still attached to it. In this spot Fedilmid, son of King Laoghaire, had his home, and his wife was a lady of Britain who, if not already a Christian, must have had some knowledge of the established religion of the empire. According to tradition, Trim was the scene of one of Patrick's most important successes.

The story goes that Lomman, one of Patrick's British fellow workers, sailed up the Boyne and landed at the ford of the Alder. In the morning Fedilmid's young son, Fortchernn, came outside and found Lomman reading the gospel. The boy immediately believed and was baptized and remained with Lomman until his mother came out to find him. She was delighted to meet a fellow countryman and she, too, believed and returned to her house and told her husband what had happened. Then Fedilmid believed. The parents consigned their son to the care of Lomman, to be his pupil and spiritual foster-child, and made a donation of their estate at Trim to Patrick and Lomman and Fortchernn.

Although the details of this story cannot be taken literally, it may preserve some of the main facts—that Fortchernn became a pupil of Lomman and embraced the spiritual life; that Fedilmid made the donation; and that the British princess played a

the first archbishop of Canterbury until his death in 604, a position that has always been considered the leader of the Church of England (Anglican Communion).

Bede's Version

The Ecclesiastical History of England (AD 731) by the Venerable Bede is one of the most important sources for our understanding of the spread of Christianity in the British islands during late antiquity and the early Middle Ages. According to Bede, Ethelbert heard something new in the message of Christian faith that he had not heard from his pagan counselors: "Sending to Ethelbert, [Augustine] signified that they were come from Rome, and brought a joyful message, which most undoubtedly assured to those that hearkened to it everlasting joys in heaven, and a kingdom that would never end, with the living and true God. The king hearing this, gave orders that they should stay in the island where they had landed, and be furnished with necessaries." Later, many years after Ethelbert's conversion, Bede felt confident enough to record the following: "In the year of our Lord 616, which is the twenty-first year after Augustine and his company were sent to preach to the English nation, Ethelbert, king of Kent, having most gloriously governed his temporal kingdom fifty-six years, entered into the eternal joys of the kingdom of Heaven. He was the third of the English kings who ruled over all the southern provinces that are divided from the northern by the river Humber and the borders contiguous to it; but the first of all that ascended to the heavenly kingdom" (Bede, I.25, II.5).

part in the episode. But tales of this kind are prone to represent happenings that were really by design as if they were by chance. It is possible that the wife of Fedilmid was already a Christian, and that, just as St. Augustine traveled to Kent by the invitation of its Gallic queen (the wife of Ethelbert), so Lomman rowed to Trim at the call of its British princess. We may be fairly certain that Lomman's coming to the ford of the Alder was not by chance, but was arranged by him and Patrick with forethought and purpose. The result was of high importance. It gave Patrick a strong position and prestige in Meath by establishing a Christian community that had associations with the son and grandson of the high-king.

Contests with Druids

The Druids were bitterly hostile to Patrick, according to the Irish imagination. The resulting scenes of Patrick's work have a spectacular effect.

He resolved to celebrate the first Easter after landing in Ireland on the hill of Slane in what is today County Meath. This hill rises high above the left bank of the River Boyne at about twelve miles from its mouth. On the night of Easter evening, he and his companions lit the paschal fire. Well, it just so happened that on that same night, the King of Ireland was holding a solemn festival in his palace at Tara where the kings and nobles of the land were gathered together. It was the custom that on such a special night no fire should be lit until one had been kindled with solemn ritual in the royal house. Suddenly, the company assembled at Tara saw a light shining across the plain of Breg from the hill of Slane, about ten miles away. King Laoghaire, surprised and alarmed, consulted with his magicians and they said, "O king, unless this fire that you see is quenched this very night, it will never be quenched. And the one who kindled it will overcome us all and seduce all the people of your realm." And the king replied, "It will not be, for we will go to see who has done this and we will put to death any who do such sin against our kingdom." And so the king had nine chariots prepared, and together with the queen and his two chief sorcerers, he drove through the night over the plain of Breg.

The magicians made preparations en route, and instructed the chariot drivers to steer continually contrary to the sun's course, turning left, in order to build their magical powers. And they urged the king not to go up to the place where the fire was kindled, or else he might be seduced into worshiping the one who kindled such a fire. Instead, they counseled that the offender should be summoned to the king's presence at a distance from the fire, so that the magicians could speak with him there.

When the company arrived at Slane they dismounted out of range of the fire and Patrick was brought to them. The sorcerers said, as he approached, "Let no one arise at his coming, for whoever rises will afterwards worship him."

When Patrick arrived and saw the chariots and horses, he quoted the words of the Psalmist, "Some take pride in chariots, and some in horses, but our pride is in the name of the LORD our God" (20:7). One of the king's company—his name was Erc—rose up when Patrick appeared and he was converted and Patrick blessed him. Then the sorcerers began to talk with Patrick and to dispute with him. Lochru, one of the enchanters, uttered strong words against the Christian faith. And Patrick, looking grimly at him, prayed to God that the blasphemer would be flung into the air and dashed to the ground. So it happened. Lochru was lifted upwards and fell on a stone, so that his head was dashed to pieces.

The king was furious and said, "Lay hands on that man!"

But Patrick, seeing the heathen about to attack him, cried out, "Let God arise, and let his enemies be scattered!"

A great darkness fell and the earth quaked, and in the tumult the Druids fell on each other and the horses fled over the plain and of all that company only the king and queen, and Lucetmael, the other sorcerer, survived.

The queen approached Patrick and said to him pleadingly, "O mighty and just man, don't destroy the king. He will come and kneel and worship your god." And the king, constrained by fear, bent his knee to Patrick and pretended to worship God. But soon afterwards, he asked Patrick to come to him, intending once again to kill him. Patrick knew his thoughts and he went before the king with his eight companions who had shared the paschal fire, one of whom was a boy. But as the king counted them, they suddenly seemed to be no longer there, but he saw in the distance eight deer and a fawn making for the wilds. And the king returned in the morning twilight to Tara, disheartened and ashamed.

The framers of this legend had an instinct for scenic effect. Consider the bold and brilliant idea of the first Easter fire flashing defiance across the plain of Meath to the heathen powers of Tara; and the vision of the king with his queen and sorcerers setting out from their palace in the deep of night with chariots and horses, careening over the plain, just as Medb and Ailill, the queen and king in the Ulster Cycle of Irish mythology, might have suddenly driven headlong against the Hound of Ulaid. Unfortunately, the calendar seems to have been disregarded by the story-makers who sometimes transfigure the facts of history. The idea is that Easter is to replace the ancient Gaelic holiday of Beltane, the Christian to overcome the heathen fire, but it seems to have been unimportant that the day of Beltane was the first day of summer (May 1), which could never fall on Easter Eve. Even more remote from the paschal season was the feast of Samhain at the close of autumn (November 1), when a fire was kindled on the Hill of Ward, also called Tlachtga, not far from Trim, and as tradition says, all of the hearths in Ireland were lit by its flame. It was at Samhain, also, that the high-kings used to hold such high festivals at Tara as the one told in our story. But even though the circumstances are incongruous, the scene is well conceived to express the triumph of the new faith. Certain, general, historical facts are embodied—namely, the hostility of the Druids and the personal distaste of the king for the foreign creed.

The story of the paschal fire has a sequel to go with it. On the following day, that is, on Easter itself, Laoghaire was feasting in his palace together with kings and princes and nobles, when

The Romance of Tara

Mystical, mythical Tara has its origins long before the time of St. Patrick. It reaches back to the Stone and Bronze Ages. The claim of the high-king to his throne was dependent, in large part, upon an ancient tradition that he "marry" the goddess Medb ("intoxicating one"), who was said to have died on the island, making it a holy place.

Patrick appeared with five of his companions. The door had been shut, but still, Patrick and his companions suddenly appeared among the king and his men—comparable, as the storyteller must have intended, to Christ appearing before the fearful disciples in the upper room in chapter 20 of John's Gospel. Patrick had come to preach the Word, and the king invited him to sit down at table. Lucetmael, the Druid, poured a poisonous drop into the cup of Patrick, in order to test him, and as the saint blessed the cup the liquor was frozen to ice, except for the drop of poison, which remained liquid and fell out when the cup was turned upside down. Then he blessed the cup again, and the drink returned to its natural state.

A little while later, the Druid said to Patrick, "Let us work miracles on the plain. Let us bring down snow on the land."

"I will not bring down anything against the will of God," Patrick replied.

But Lucetmael persisted, and by his incantations he brought snow that was waist high on the ground.

"Now remove it," said the saint.

"I cannot," Lucetmael said, "until this same time tomorrow."

"You can do evil, but not good," Patrick replied, and as he blessed the plain the snow vanished without rain or mist or wind. Everyone present applauded and marveled. Then, in the same way as before, the Druid brought darkness down on the earth, but he could not dissipate it, and Patrick did so.

At this point in the testing, the high-king Laoghaire said to Patrick and Lucetmael, "Dip your books in water and we will worship he whose books come out dry." Patrick was willing to accept this test, but the sorcerer refused on the grounds that Patrick worshiped water as a god, meaning its use in baptism. Then the king proposed the same test with fire instead of water, but the Druid said, "No, this man worships fire and water alternately."

And so, finally, Patrick proposed an ordeal, which was accepted. His pupil Benignus and the magician were placed in a hut built half of green and half of dry, wood. Benignus, clothed in the magician's garment, was placed in the dry part, and Lucetmael, wearing the garment of Patrick, in the green part. The hut was set on fire in the presence of everyone. Then Patrick prayed, and the fire consumed the magician, leaving Patrick's robe unburned, but it did not hurt Benignus, even though it burned the magician's robe from round about his body. At this, Laoghaire was tempted to kill Patrick, but he was afraid.

A similar story, with an instructive parallel, is the famous one about the funeral pyre of King Croesus, mentioned above. The fundamental motive of that story was the burning of the lion god Sandan, but the incident has been changed into a historical context so as to disguise its origin, and the tale was largely accepted as literal fact. But Croesus was as innocent of dooming his defeated foe to a cruel death as Patrick was of burning his Druid rival. In both cases, the true victims of the legendary flames were the spirits of popular imagination.

The story bears the stamp of an early origin. It is a common fallacy that legends attach themselves to a figure only after a long lapse of time, and that the antiquity of biographies may always be measured by the presence or absence of miracles. The truth is that those people who are destined to become the subjects of myth evoke the myth-making instinct in others while they are still alive, or before they are cold in their graves. The myths that are significant and characteristic are nearly contemporary; they arise within the radius of the personality to which they relate. The tale of Patrick's first Easter in Ireland and his dealings with the king is certainly a creation of this kind.

Nevertheless, in this legend of Patrick's dealings with the high-king there is one implication that harmonizes with other records. Patrick visited Laoghaire in his palace at Tara, but he went as a guest in peace, not as a hostile magician and a destroyer of life. Laoghaire agreed to protect Patrick in his own kingdom, although he resisted any attempts that were made to convert him. No cross would be raised over his sepulcher; he would be buried, like his forefathers, standing and dressed in his arms.

Still, the place of the Christian communities in Irish society raised questions that could not be settled without a general conclave of the kings and chieftains of the island. They must get together to discuss what would be the rights and obligations, the modifications of existing customs and laws, the principles and doctrines, that this new religion demanded. Now, it was a custom of the high-kings to hold an occasional great celebration, called the Feast of Tara, to which the under-kings were all invited. This was an opportunity for discussing the common affairs of the realm. Such an occasion is evidently contemplated in the legend, and the annals record that a Feast of Tara was held towards the close of Laoghaire's reign. It is therefore possible that at such an assembly the religious questions were marked as subjects for deliberation, and the bishop was invited to be present. If so, the general issue of the debate must have been that Christian communities were recognized as social units on the same footing as families, but that Christian principles shouldn't alter the general principles of Irish law.

Laoghaire had done for Ireland what Euric did for the Visigoths, Gundobad for the Burgundians, and Clovis for the Salian Franks. The idea of compiling a written legal code had probably come from the Roman Empire. In light of this, it would have been natural that the Christian bishop and also a Roman citizen, who represented more than any other man in Ireland the ideas of Roman civilization, would have been consulted. But there was another reason why Patrick would naturally have been taken into the counsels of the kings and lawyers. The spread of Christianity and the foundation of Christian communities throughout the land rendered it imperative for the secular authorities to define the status of the clergy and fix the law that should be binding on everyone. A new society had been established, recognizing laws of its own that differed from the laws of the country, and this threatened to create a double system that would have struck a fatal blow to order. Either the spirit of the Mosaic law must be allowed to transform the ancient customs of the land, or the Christians must resign themselves to living under principles opposed to ecclesiastical teaching.

It is possible that Patrick made an attempt to revolutionize the Irish system of dealing with cases of manslaughter, to abolish the customs of private retaliation, and make it an offense punishable by death. But if he made such an attempt it was unsuccessful, and it probably would have received little support from his native converts. The principle of primitive societies that blood-shedding was a private offense that could be atoned for by payment of some sort—a principle that Greek societies were discarding in the seventh century BC—prevailed in Ireland so long as Ireland was independent, and the Irish Church seemed to be perfectly content.

CHAPTER TEN

Early Conversions and Communities

"Had Ireland possessed cities after the Continental model, St. Patrick would undoubtedly have made them centers of ecclesiastical government, following the invariable practice since the first days of the Church. But cities were not forthcoming; the dun of the ruling prince could not be used, since it was his private dwelling-place; and points of vantage like the hills of assembly could not be occupied because of the traditional purpose which they served. . . . As the bishop everywhere else in Christendom ruled in a civitas, so conversely the seats of ecclesiastical rule in Ireland, though not civitates in the Latin sense, came to be known by that term. In the Patrician documents the word is used of Armagh, Slane. . . . At a later period the word was applied in a wider sense to any important monastery, and again by a further extension to places of assembly like Tara. These primitive ecclesiastical 'cities' were probably diminutive in size." (Ryan, 88)

Many of the early traditions of communities founded by Patrick are to be trusted. Within Laoghaire's own immediate kingdom many churches claimed to have been founded by him, one or two of them in the neighborhood of the royal hill. But although the names of the places where these churches were built are recorded, they are in most cases only names to us; the sites cannot be identified and must be only guessed at. In a few places in the land of Meath we can localize the literary traditions. We may begin with a church that was founded not by the bishop himself, but by a disciple and, it was believed, a relative. Not far south from Tara lies Dunshaughlin, and the name is intended to convey Domnach Sechnaill, "the church of

Seachnaill." Seachnaill, or Secundinus, his Latin name, is supposed to have been Patrick's nephew. It is very difficult to accept his alleged relationship to Patrick, but as the tradition goes, Seachnaill composed the first Latin hymn of Ireland, and the theme of the hymn was the apostolic work of his master. It is composed in trochaic rhythm, but with almost complete disregard for metrical quantity or literary merit, and its twenty-three quatrains begin with the successive letters of the alphabet.

The Hymn of St. Seachnaill

"The Hymn of St. Seachnaill," as it is known, is mostly frustrating for the historian. Patrick is spoken of throughout as if he were alive, but there are no references to particular acts of the saint or episodes in his life. For this reason, it was probably written before Patrick's death. There is no mention of miracles. The author seems to have confined himself to generalities, and the Hymn supplies no real material for Patrick's biography. Nevertheless, it is of value to us. It is among the earliest memorials that we possess of his work, and if it was written by Seachnaill, it was written before Patrick had been in Ireland for fourteen years. The writer may have derived his inspiration from Patrick's own impressions about his work. We may suspect that some of the verses echo words that had fallen from Patrick's lips in the presence of his disciple, as when the master is compared to Paul, or described as a fisherman setting his nets for the heathen, or called the light of the world, or a witness of God *in lege catholica* ("by his Catholic teaching"). But Seachnaill did not live to see the fuller realization of Patrick's claims to the laudations of his hymn. The disciple died sometime in 447–448, long before the master had finished his "perfect life."

Donagh-Patrick and Laoghaire's Brother

In another district of Meath, near the banks of the River Blackwater, the town of Donagh-Patrick seems to mark a spot associated with one of Patrick's important successes. It was there that Conall, the son of Niall and brother of High-King Laoghaire, had his dwelling. The place is still marked by the foundations of an ancient fort, and Conall seems to have been more receptive to the persuasions of Patrick's teaching than his greater brother was. Conall submitted to the rite of baptism and granted a place, close to his own house, for the building of a church. Patrick measured out the ground and a church of unusual size rose up which was twenty yards from end to end, and it was known as the Great Church of Patrick. Such was the scale of the early houses of Christian worship in Ireland.

More about the Hymn

"We are indebted to the Irish Archaeological Society for an elegant and accurate edition of the original text of this hymn of St. Seachnaill. . . . St. Patrick is described as: 'keeping the blessed command of Christ in all things: his good works shine illustrious before men, who, following his holy and wonderful example, thus magnify as their Lord the Father who is in heaven. He was sent by God to fish with the nets of faith, and thus draw the believers from the world unto grace. The chosen Gospel talents of Christ were dispensed by him with usury amongst the Irish people. He preached by works as well as by words, and stimulated to holiness by his example. He was humble in spirit and in body, and in his flesh bore the stigmata of Christ, in whose cross alone he glorified, being sustained by its saving power. He feeds the faithful with the heavenly banquet lest they should faint in the way of the commandments of Christ. . . . He prays daily for the sins of his people, and offers in their behalf the sacrifice worthy of God. He is a faithful witness to the

Lord by his Catholic teaching. He chants the hymns, the Apocalypse, the Psalms, and expounds them for the instruction of the people.'" (Moran, 90–91)

The conversion of Conall was an important achievement, but there were other sons of Niall who were so bitterly averse to the new faith that they appear to have plotted to take the life of its teacher. Not far from the place where he won the friendship of Conall, Patrick had been in danger of his life at the hands of Coirpre, Conall's brother. Above the confluence of the Blackwater with the Boyne, the village of Telltown remembers the memory of Taillte, a place of great fame in ancient Meath. It was there that a fair was held and a feast celebrating the beginning of autumn; people gathered together to witness the games that were held, perhaps under the presidency of the high-king. The record of the visit of Patrick to Taillte mentions the games as the "royal agon," an allusion to ancient Greek comedy. It is not clear whether Patrick is supposed to have timed his visit to see and denounce the heathen usages of the festival. Perhaps, instead, he would have avoided such an occasion with discretion, waiting outside the town until the pagan people had finished their celebrations. The story is that Coirpre, son of King Niall, wished to put Patrick to death at Taillte, and punished his servants because they would not betray their master into his hands.

But if the bishop was in danger from a son of Niall at Taillte, he is said to have fared worse at the hands of a grandson of Niall at another venerable place in the kingdom of Meath. The hill of Uisnech, in southwestern Meath, was believed to mark the center of the island and was a scene of pagan worship. Patrick visited the hill town, and a stone known as the "stone of Coithrige"—perhaps a sacred stone on which he inscribed a cross—commemorated his name and his visit. The stone has disappeared now, but the traveler is reminded of it by the stone enclosure that is known as "St. Patrick's bed." While he was there, a grandson of Niall murdered some of his foreign companions. Patrick cursed both the grandson and Coirpre, and foretold that no king should ever spring from their seed, but that their posterity would serve the posterity of their brothers. Tradition continually shows Patrick as a proponent of malediction.

Proceeding from Donagh-Patrick up the River Blackwater, Patrick came to the ford of the Quern and planted another Christian settlement, there. This place was probably near the old town of Kells. Unlike Trim, Kells has some traces of the early age of Christian Ireland, although with nothing to claim association with the age of Patrick. The ancient stone house that is preserved there is connected by tradition with the name of the great saint Columba who, a hundred years after Patrick's death, went forth from Ireland to convert northern Britain.

Patrick established other churches, as well, in the northwestern region of Meath. The River Ethne, which is now pronounced Inny, flows through this region to contribute its waters to a swelling of the River Shannon. We are told that from the hill of Granard he pointed out to one of his followers the spot where a church should be founded. This church, Cell Raithin, may have been the origin of the settlement that grew into the town of Granard. Among those who came to live in the monastery that was established in Granard, there is one who had a special, interesting connection with Patrick's life. Gosact, described as the son of his old master, Miliucc, was, according to tradition, ordained there as a priest by the captive stranger who had once cared for his father's herds. The tomb of Gosact seems to have been a place of pilgrimage at Granard during the Middle Ages. It is questionable whether or not Gosact was actually a son of Miliucc, Patrick's former master, but he may nonetheless have been connected with those years of bondage.

The Idol of Mag Slecht

Having done what he could towards planting the faith in Tethbia, Patrick took himself northward to one of the chief strongholds and sanctuaries of pagan worship in all Ireland. In the plain of Slecht, in a region that belonged to the kingdom of Connaught (falling now in the province of Ulster), was a famous idol. It was apparently a stone, covered with silver and gold, standing in a sacred circle, surrounded by twelve pillar-stones. This idol was known as Cenn Cruaich or Crom Cruaich, and its worship was common even among the British Celts across the sea. The precinct of Mag Slecht was a national center of pagan religion in the days of Patrick. Some said that the firstborn, even of human offspring, were once offered to this idol in order to secure a plenteous yield of corn and milk, and that the high-kings of Ireland themselves used to come at the beginning of winter to do worship there.

If the cult possessed such national significance, it would have been one of Patrick's greatest feats if he assaulted and conquered its powers. The story goes that he came and struck down the idol with his staff. If this happened, if the golden pillar of the older god was thus cast down by the servant of the new divinity, it must have been done with the consent of the secular powers. This would have marked, more than any other single event, the formal success of Christian aggression against the pagan spirit of Ireland. The blow struck by Patrick at the stone of Mag Slecht would have been as the stroke of Boniface at the oak of Geismar. The fall of Cenn Cruaich would have been as illustrious in the story of the spread of Christianity in the island of the Scots as was the fall of the Irmin pillar on a Westphalian hill in the advance of Christendom from the Rhine River to the River Elbe under the banner of Charlemagne. The apostle of the Irish would have justly and proudly sent some fragment of the fallen image to the Roman pontiff, a trophy of the victory of their faith.

In a later age, the apostle to the Baltic Slavs sent to Rome the three-headed god he took from the temple of

Chopping Down Paganism

Bury mentions two of the greatest apostles to the Germans: King Charlemagne, who brought Christianity by military force, and St. Boniface, the patron saint of Germany. St. Boniface (d. 754) cut down "the oak of Geismar," also known as "Thor's oak," in order to eliminate a pagan symbol that was worshiped by the local people. For this reason, iconography of Boniface usually pictures him holding an axe. "Irmin" is the name of another ancient Germanic god, and the Irmin pillar mentioned by Bury was the name of an actual oak tree in Westphalia that stood as a pagan location for connection of heaven and earth. When Charles the Great (d. 814), also known as Charlemagne, King of the Franks, conquered this region, he brought Christianity to the pagans.

Stettin to show the head of the church how a new land was being won for Christ. But the truth is that the episode of Cenn Cruaich, even though the incident rests on an ancient tradition, held little prominence in the oldest records of St. Patrick. We may suppose that the worship of the idol was of interest only to the surrounding regions and had no national importance for the island as a whole. If Patrick suppressed the worship and cast down the god, it was simply one of his local successes, one of many victories in his struggle with heathenism, rather than a crowning triumph.

CHAPTER ELEVEN

Preaching and Legends in Connaught

Christians Before Patrick's Arrival

Some scholars have argued that the rapid growth of Christianity during Patrick's three decades in Ireland must have happened because there were many British Christians already there, before the saint's arrival. This runs contrary, however, to Muirchu's seventh-century *Life of St. Patrick*. Muirchu described the features of what both Patrick and Palladius were to encounter upon arriving in Ireland: a cold northern climate and similarly cold and harsh people, disinclined to accept any new teaching.

We remember how the cry of the children of Fochlad, heard by Patrick in visions and dreams at night, was the supreme call he felt in returning to Ireland. Although his outlook must have widened as he came face to face with facts upon his arrival, and new tasks of great importance and timeliness presented themselves, enlarging the conception of his work as he had originally grasped it, we shouldn't doubt that to make his way to the forest of Fochlad was still the most cherished wish of his heart. It is uncertain exactly how long Patrick had been in the island before he set out to accomplish this desire. However much he found to do in Ulidia and Meath, Patrick would probably have moved steadily toward his goal of preaching the gospel in the western parts of Connaught.

The land of King Amolngaid, in north Mayo, was one district away from the woods of Fochlad. Patrick was at work there approximately thirteen or fourteen years into his work in

Ireland. The king couldn't be persuaded to allow the new religion entry. We are told that Patrick crossed the River Shannon and visited Connaught three times during his lifetime, and so, it is possible that he penetrated to Fochlad—the region he had known as a slave—earlier, but not in a meaningful way. In the records, events that belong to different journeys are thrown together and it isn't often possible to distinguish them. But this chronological uncertainty does not seriously affect the view of Patrick's labors in Connaught as they were remembered there.

Patrick founded many churches in many towns in this region beyond the River Shannon. If we are right in supposing that this was the region in which Patrick spent the years of his captivity, then the church he founded in the town of Aghagower may hold a singular interest. Of all the churches he founded in Ireland, this one perhaps more than any other fulfilled his wish to use his life for these people. It would have been in this place, west of the lake country of Mayo and Galway, and west of Carra, that he revisited the scenes where he had herded his master's flocks and prayed at night in the woods in snow and rain. Here he again climbed the mountain that he describes from his days of bondage and which was always afterwards to be linked with his name. Crochan Aigli—which is now called Croagh Patrick—rises high and prominently on the north shore of the wild and desolate promontory, girt on three sides by the sea, known as the "sea-land."

Patrick retired for lonely contemplation and prayer to the summit of this peak. It is said that he remained there, fasting for forty days and forty nights, like the Jewish teachers Moses, Elijah, and Jesus. Many lives of saints were once written self-consciously to seek the similitudes to the stories of Moses and other holy men of the Christian scriptures; however, it is also conceivable that the similitude was designed by Patrick himself. If he desired a season of isolation to commune with his own soul and meditate on invisible things, Patrick may have fixed the term of his retreat by the highest examples. The forty days and forty nights may be the literal truth, and may have helped to move the imagination of his disciples to create a legend. In later days, people imagined the saint encompassed by the company of the saints of Ireland. According to these legends, God said to the souls of the saints, not only of the dead and living, but of those still unborn, "Go up, O ye saints, to the top of the mountain that is higher than all the other mountains of the west, and bless the people of Ireland." Then the souls mounted, and they flitted round the lofty peak (although, not the loftiest; Mount Nephin, close to Lake Conn, is higher) in the form of birds, darkening the air, so great was their multitude. And so it goes that God heartened Patrick by revealing to him the fruit to come of these labors.

Ever since those days, this western mountain has been associated with St. Patrick, not only bearing his name, but drawing multitudes of pilgrims to it. Every year, on the anniversary of his death, they come and toil up the steep ascent of Croagh Patrick. The confined space of its summit is the one spot where we feel some assurance that we stand literally in his footsteps and realize that, as we look southward over the desolate moors and tarns of Murrisk, beyond the islets to the spaces of the ocean, we are viewing a scene on which Patrick's eye looked for many days. But the spot has a greater interest if it is associated with both his solitary retreat, and the servitude of his boyhood. The meditations on the mount were infused with emotions intelligible to the children of reason, those of us who may not understand the need of "saints" for fasting and prayer. It requires little imagination to realize what the man's feelings must have been when he returned to the places of his slavery, conscious that he was now a "light among the Gentiles," and that his bitter captivity had led to such great results. Both human and saintly impulses led Patrick to seek isolation on the mountain where he had first turned to thoughts of religion amid the herds of his heathen lord.

The Seat of the Kings of Connaught

Bishop Patrick's journey continued to the fortress of Crochan, the ancient seat of the kings of Connaught. The royal palace stood on one of the highest and broadest of the low ridges that mark the plain of Ai, and although, as in the case of the other palaces of the kings of Ireland, no remains of the habitation survive except the earthen structure, it is quite something to stand there. This is the site of Rathcroghan, where Queen Medb and her lords lived, that is, if they ever lived at all. Around the royal fort itself the ground is covered with other mounds and raths and memorials of ancient history, so that one can hardly imagine what appearance Crochan presented to Patrick. Sepulchers were near at hand, a place that the kings would visit from their stronghold, just as the kings of Mycenae went down from their citadel to the tombs below. In that field of the dead one red stone stands conspicuous to the present day, and the uncertain tradition is that it marks the tomb of Dathi, the successor and nephew of Niall and the last pagan king of Ireland. If there is any truth to this tradition, the pillar would be an interesting link with the age of Patrick, for it would have been set up only a few years before he visited the place.

Imagination filled many spots of Ireland with supernatural beings—not only with fairies, but also with earth-folk that were once at least human. Gaelic mythology tells of the Tuatha De Danann, people of the goddess Danu, who were believed to have colonized the island of Ireland, and to have eventually been conquered by the Milesians. Driven from the surface of the ground, they found new homes in chambered mounds where they practiced their magical

Splendid Pagan Ruins

Rathcroghan is a site of prehistoric ruins. Standing stones and old burial grounds cover the area. This place links the early Bronze Age (the fourth millennium BC) to the era of the birth of Christianity in that area; it is associated with pagan royalty, like Tara. An early Christian poet of Ireland once wrote, "Although destroyed, paganism was everywhere and splendid; it is now only cities without worship." Rathcroghan was one of these places.

crafts. No spot was more closely associated with these fabled beings than the hill of Rathcroghan. On ground so alive with legend, in a place that stimulated fancy, it was impossible that the incident of Patrick's visit should be handed down in the sober colors of history, or that it would escape the meshes of fable. But the legend-shaping instinct of some Christian poet wrought here with signal grace, and the story must have been invented within decades of Patrick's visit.

The Rathcroghan Legend

The tale tells that Patrick and the bishops who were with him had assembled together at a fountain near Rathcroghan to hold a council before sunrise. Two maidens came down to wash at the fountain. They were the daughters of the high-king of

Ireland, and their names were Ethne the White and Fedelm the Red. They lived at Crochan, to be fostered and educated by two Druids, Mael and Caplait. These Druids had been deeply alarmed when they heard that Patrick was about to cross the River Shannon, and by their sorceries they had brought darkness and mist down over the plain of Ai to hinder him from entering the land. The darkness of night prevailed for three straight days, but was finally dispelled by the saint's prayers.

When the princesses saw the bishops and priests sitting around the fountain, they were amazed at their strange garb, and did not know what to think of them. Were they fairies? Or were they earth-folk? Or were they an illusion, an unreal vision? And so they accosted the strangers and asked, "Where have you come from? And where is your home?"

Patrick answered, "It would be better for you to believe in the true God whom we worship than to ask questions about our race."

"Who is God, where is God, and who's god is he?" the eldest girl precociously responded. And then she continued, "Where does he live? Does he have sons and daughters, your God? Does he have gold and silver? Is he immortal? Is he fair? Is he in heaven or in earth, in the sea, in the rivers, in the hill places, in the valleys? Tell us how we may know him. How is he discovered?"

To all of this, Patrick replied, "Our God is the God of all people, the God of heaven and earth, of seas and rivers, of sun and moon and stars, of the lofty mountain and the lowly valley, the God above heaven and in heaven and under heaven. He has his dwelling around heaven and earth and sea and all that is in them. He inspires every thing; he gives life to all; he supports all. He lights the light of the sun, and furnishes the light of the night. He has a Son co-eternal with himself, and like unto himself. The Son is not younger than the Father, and the Father is not older than the Son. And the Holy Spirit breathes in them. The Father, Son, and Spirit are undivided. I wish to unite you with the heavenly king, as you are daughters of an earthly king. Believe!"

The princesses were rapt. Together, they said, "Tell us how we may believe in the heavenly king that we may see him face to face. We will do as you say."

And so Patrick brought them into the faith. He said, "Do you believe that by baptism you can cast away the sin of your father and mother?" "We believe," the women said. "Do you believe in repentance after sin?" "We believe." "Do you believe in life after death?" "We believe." "Do you believe in the resurrection in the day of judgment?" "We believe." "Do you believe in the unity of the church?" "We believe."

Patrick then baptized them in the fountain and placed a white veil on their heads, and they begged that they might behold the face of Christ. Patrick said, "Until you taste of death, you cannot see the face of Christ, and unless you receive the sacrifice." They answered him, "Give us the sacrifice so that we may see the Son, our bridegroom." And they received the Eucharist, then fell asleep in death, and were placed in one bed together where their friends came to mourn them.

Then Caplait the Druid came, and Patrick preached to him, and he too believed and became a monk. His brother Mael was angry with Caplait for falling away, and hoped to recall him to the old faith, but on hearing Patrick's teaching he too became a Christian and his head was tonsured.

When the prescribed days of lamentation for the king's daughters were over, the maidens were buried in a round tomb near the fountain. Their grave was dedicated to God and to Patrick and his heirs after him, and he constructed a church of earth in that place.

Throughout this curious legend is embedded some matters of historical significance. First, the motive for the legend of the two virgins who died in the hour of their conversion recurs in other tales, as well. There is the story of Ros, brother of Dichu, told in the story of the life of St. Brendan, but more important, perhaps, is the parallel story from elsewhere in the legends of St. Patrick. The same thing is told in Muirchu's story of Monesan, daughter of a king of Britain, who could not be induced by her parents to marry, and persisted in asking her mother and her nurse eternal questions. Her parents, hearing that Patrick received weekly visits from God, took her to Ireland and sought the saint to allow their daughter to see God. He baptized her, and she immediately committed her spirit to the hands of the angels. She was buried at a church that Muirchu doesn't name, but her relics were venerated there in his own day.

Second, there is solid basis of fact for a tomb by the spring of Rathcroghan. At that tomb the story grew up that when they were baptized, the desire of the maidens for the heavenly vision was fulfilled immediately by their death. This legend was then worked up artificially, and the dialogue was composed and written down in Irish, partly in verse. The freshness and simplicity are striking, and some particulars justify the supposition that this happened at an early date, within the first generation after St. Patrick's death. The naïve wonder of the young women at the appearance of the clerks, the brief view that Patrick unfolds of the articles of his religion, the emphasis laid upon the unity of the church—all point to the conclusion that the story took shape when Patrick's way of teaching, and the first impressions made upon pagans by the apostles of the new faith, were still fresh in the memory of the faithful. The dialogue is artificial, for the questions of the damsels are arranged so as to lead up to the bishop's exposition of his creed. The baptismal questions of Patrick also assume a certain knowledge that is inconsistent with that of people who have just heard the message for the first time.

If it is true that the legend originated at an early date and was cast into literary shape at least before the end of the fifth century, we can then infer that the maidens were indeed the daughters of Laoghaire. It is unlikely that the women would have been so identified by an invention of popular legend, nor by any recorder of Patrick's acts, living within a generation of his death. By sending his children away, to be raised away from home, Laoghaire would have been following the general practice in the country at that time. And that he would have sent them to the royal residence of Connaught would have been good sense. The fathers of King Amolngaid and King Laoghaire were brothers, and it would not be surprising that Laoghaire would send his daughters to Rathcroghan to be educated by the Druids of Amolngaid.

The Druid brothers are also of great interest to us, as their names hint at the tensions between the native faith of the fifth century and the Roman traditions, which did not become normative in Ireland until a couple of centuries later. Mael's Irish name means "tonsured one" and designates that he had what became a native Celtic tonsure, by which only the front part of the head was shaven from ear to ear. Caplait's Latin name, meanwhile, derives from *capillatus*, or "de-capillated, shorn," and signifies the removal of all the hair in the fashion that was already in practice in the western empire; this latter method became known as the Roman tonsure. We know that in the seventh century the Celtic tonsure prevailed in the Irish and British churches, and this was one of the chief questions in the Roman controversy. The conclusion has been generally drawn that the Roman tonsure was not known in Ireland until the victory of the Roman party in the seventh century.

Both Druids were tonsured by Patrick according to the story; both, it is implied, wore the native tonsure until they were converted. The name "Caplait" couldn't have been applied to either of them until after his conversion. But when they became monks it applied equally to both, just as "Mael" was equally applicable to both when they were still Druids. Thus the story, taken literally, does not hang together, and the transparent names suggest that it arose from some other circumstances. The story was actually told in order to explain the existence of a proverb: *cosmail Mael do Chaplait*, "Mael is like unto Caplait." We may infer that the Christian tonsure had been introduced and enforced by Patrick, but that his rule was relaxed and disregarded after his death, as the native clergy adopted the old native tonsure of the Druids. The two fashions subsisted side by side for a while, then the Roman tonsure fell completely out of use, until it was restored in the seventh century. But the proverb arose when the two tonsures were in use together, and expressed the claim that the native mode was as legitimate for a monk as the foreign.

More Churches and Converts

From Rathcroghan, Patrick and his company proceeded westward and planted religious foundations in the region that is now most easily described as the barony of Castlereagh. A number of Gallic clergy traveled with him, and these he dispersed to found other churches in other places. One of these was known as Baslic, a name that survives as the name of a parish, preserving the memory of the foreign clergy who thought of the greater *basilicae* of the empire when they built their little sanctuary in the wilds of Connaught and gave it the high-sounding name of *Basilica sanctorum*. No place name in Ireland, due to Christianity, has a greater interest than Basilica, west of Rathcroghan. Another church founded in this region, near the banks of the River Suck, was Cell Garad, which is perhaps to be sought at Oran, where an old burial ground and the fragment of a belfry mark an ancient ecclesiastical site. Both Baslic and Cell Garad were the seats of bishops.

What Happened in the Seventh Century?

Bury mentions that the Roman tonsure became the norm for Christian monks in the seventh century, but he doesn't explain the connection. It is simple: the Synod of Whitby. Whitby is the site of an abbey in Northumbria, Britain, which played host to an important medieval, church-wide meeting of bishops in Britain and Ireland, in 664. Until that time, Christian practice existed in two forms of liturgical traditions: the native Celtic and Ionan (inspired by monks on the island of Iona) in Ireland and Britain, respectively, and the Roman. The Roman practices were normative throughout the western churches, following the customs of Rome. It was primarily the dating of Easter and the tonsure that were discussed at Whitby, and the Roman practices won out.

Patrick then went northward and westward, baptizing converts and founding churches along his way. Eventually we come to a journey for which we have a definite, chronological foundation, since we know that it was undertaken soon after the death of King Amolngaid, and he died sometime around thirteen years after Patrick's arrival in Ireland. This story represents the land

Training Priests in Ireland

There were no Irish seminaries until the modern era. The tradition had always been to send men seeking to become priests to the European continent, usually to France, for their schooling in canon law, theology, and philosophy, leaving people with the clear impression that Irish Catholicism was reliant upon Rome. The narrator of Patrick Kavanagh's autobiographical novel, *Tarry Flynn*, says of the local parish priest in familiar fashion, "Father Daly was a fine cut of a man; he had been educated at Rome and Louvain and was full of a pedantic scholasticism which he somehow managed to relate to the needs of the people" (Kavanagh, 14). But after the French Revolution in 1789, when most of the religious institutions were seized or shut down, the Catholic Church in Ireland felt the need to begin a national seminary. An act of the Irish Parliament created the Roman Catholic College of St. Patrick in 1795. Today, the school is called St. Patrick's College Maynooth, and more than 11,000 priests have been ordained there.

of Amolngaid as the region of Fochlad that had been the goal of Patrick's desires.

Near the palace of King Laoghaire at Tara, Patrick overheard a conversation between two noblemen, one of whom was Endae, son of Amolngaid, come from the far west, "from Mag Domnon and the wood of Fochlad." Then Patrick, hearing the magical name of his dream, was thrilled with joy. Turning around, he cried to Endae, "I will go with you, if it's the last thing I do, for God has told me to go!"

Endae replied, "You cannot come with me, for we would be slain together."

"However," Patrick prophesied, "you will never reach your home alive if I do not travel with you. Also, you will never find eternal life. It is on my account that you have come this far."

"Baptize my son, for he is young," Endae said, "but I and my brothers may not believe in you until we come to our own people, or else they would mock us." So Patrick baptized his son Conall.

It appears that Endae and his six brothers had come to Tara to invoke the judgment of the high-king in a dispute about the inheritance of their father's property. The claim of Endae and his son was opposed to the claim of the other six. In passing judgment, King Laoghaire is said to have invited Patrick's aid, and they decided that the inheritance should be divided among the brothers in seven parts. This was a decision in favor of Endae's brothers, if we may suppose that Endae's claim was for the division to be eightfold, to include his son Conall. But however this may have been, Endae is said to have dedicated his seventh portion and his son Conall to Patrick and to Patrick's God.

Patrick set out with Endae and his brothers, and having crossed at a ford of the River Moy, they entered the territory of Amolngaid, where the woods of Fochlad were to be found. Beyond, and to the west, were the wilds of Mag Domnon. It should not surprise us that the coming of the Christian teacher and the baptism of Conall would arouse wrath and disgust among the Druids. And there may be some historical foundation for the legend that tells how the chief Druid, Rechrad, sought to kill Patrick. Along with nine other Druids, all arrayed in white, he advanced to meet Endae and his company. When Endae saw them, he snatched up his arms to drive them off, but Patrick raised his left hand and cursed the wizard, and Rechrad fell dead. The other Druids fled into Mag Domnon; and when the people saw this miracle, many were baptized.

It was according to this legend that Christianity entered the northern regions of Fochlad. Near the forest and close to the seashore, a church was founded, and not far from it a cross was set up. The local name for this place is Crosspatrick.

There is an old churchyard and traces of ruins, to the right of the road from Ballina to Killala, a mile south of Killala. The original church, which was surely built of timber, was to be overshadowed afterwards by the neighboring foundation of Killala, conspicuous by its lofty belfry. Elsewhere, Patrick had a square church of earth constructed, at the gathering place of the sons of Amolngaid, that may be identified with Mullafarry, "the hill of the meeting place."

Did Patrick Even Exist?

Some scholars have argued that St. Patrick, in fact, never really existed. They say that the Irish needed to create a powerful founder in order to glorify the origin of their church. Perhaps, they suggest, the Patrick power and legends were invented and placed upon the life of a much more ordinary missionary by that name. Bury obviously disagrees with this argument; but one of his contemporaries, Heinrich Zimmer, wrote as follows: "It would not require a long stretch of imagination if we assume that, about 625, Ireland's pious wish of having an apostle of her own was realized by reviving the memory of this Patricius, who had been forgotten everywhere except in the southeast. It was in this way, I think, that the Patrick legend sprang up with its two chief premises: first, that Ireland was entirely pagan in 432, as the lands of the Picts and of the Saxons had been in 563 and 597 respectively; and secondly, that Patrick converted Ireland within a short time and introduced a Christian Church, overcoming all obstacles and winning the favor of King Laoghaire, incidents analogous to Columba's conversion of King Brude, or Augustine's of Ethelbert of Kent" (Zimmer, 80).

CHAPTER TWELVE
Visit to Rome

Patrick may have intended to visit Rome long before he began his labors in Ireland. We are told by Muirchu that, before his ordination as bishop, Patrick had left his home in Britain for the purpose of visiting Rome, to receive instruction there for his life work in Ireland. But he halted on his way at Auxerre, and remained there "at the feet" of Germanus. In any case, if Patrick entertained thoughts of visiting the holy city, it seems that circumstances hindered him from realizing them until sometime between AD 441–443.

It would have been natural for Patrick to cherish the idea of visiting the center of western Christendom. And we might expect that when he had spent some years in the toil and disappointment, alternating hope and fear, successes and defeats, which are part of missionary work in a barbarous land, he would have wished to receive some recognition for his work and sympathy for his efforts from the head of the western churches. He might have counted on finding sympathy and encouragement. The interest of the Roman see was clear in the sending of Palladius, but we cannot be sure whether or not Patrick ever received a message himself from the successor of Pope Celestine I (AD 422–432).

There was another motive for visiting Rome, as well. Patrick was the son of his age, and as such, he surely recognized the high importance of the relics of the saints, especially of the early apostles, Sts. Paul and Peter, located there. He may even have thought of acquiring some special relics for his return to the churches of Ireland. The religious estimation of relics had

The Cult of Saints

The first Christian communities were embattled, often living in persecution in the Roman Empire, and for various reasons feeling that they were in the "end times" spoken about by Jesus and in scripture. By the middle of the third century, however, these eschatological anticipations had lapsed, the Roman emperor had himself been converted, and a worldwide Christian movement was being built. With it grew what has come to be called "the cult of saints"—that is, the identification of exemplary Christians who had been martyred, the preserving of their relics, the establishing of places where they should be venerated, and the spreading of their teachings.

become common in the fourth century. Such a learned man as Gregory of Nyssa set great importance in them. We could discuss this subject at great length, but it will suffice to remind the reader of the excitement that was caused in the religious world in the year 386 when Ambrose of Milan discovered the tombs of Sts. Gervasius and Protasius. The bishops of the west vied for shares in the remains. In Gaul, three cities—Tours, Rouen, and Vienne—were fortunate enough to receive scraps of linen or particles of blood-stained dust that had touched the precious bodies. It is certain that Patrick must have shared in this universal reverence for relics, and could not have failed to deem it an object of high importance to secure such things of value for his church. The hope of winning a fragment of a cerement cloth or some grains of dust would have been a big inducement to visit Rome, the city of many martyrs.

Patrick had been in Ireland for eight years when a greater pope than Celestine I or Sixtus III was elected to the see of Rome. The pontificate of Leo the Great began in 440, and marks an eminent station in the progress of the Roman bishops to the commanding position that they were ultimately to occupy in Europe. His path had been prepared by his forerunners, but it was he who induced the emperor to make a formal and imperial sanction to the religious authority of the Roman see in the west. Leo also plays a more leading and decisive part than any of his predecessors in molding Christian theology by his famous epistle on the occasion of the Council of Chalcedon (AD 451). Leo took a direct and energetic interest in the extension of the borders of Christendom, more so than his predecessors had done.

It was in the year after his elevation that Patrick

Leo and the Council of Chalcedon

Pope Leo I wrote an epistle to Flavian, the bishop of Constantinople, that became the basis for settling an argument that had grown up between the Christian churches of the east and west about how the divine and human natures were combined in the personhood of Christ. "He composed a treatise on the Incarnation . . . teaching that in Christ there are two natures, human and divine, unmixed and unconfused, yet permanently and really united in a single person, so that it is possible to attribute to the humanity of Jesus all the actions and attributes of his divinity, and vice versa." This became one of the most important early occasions when the conclusions of the bishop of Rome became for the western churches at large the "word" of God on earth (Duffy, 45).

probably took himself to Rome. No step could have been more natural, and none could have been more politic. It was equally wise whether or not he was assured of the good will of Leo beforehand. He must have wanted to report the success of his labors to the head of the western churches, of which Ireland was the youngest. He wanted to enlist Leo's sympathy, gain his

---

Pope St. Leo the Great

Pope Leo the Great (440–461) was the most important pope of late antiquity. He was the one who solidified the authority of the bishop of Rome as the leader of the Western Church, and he had a fervent missionary spirit. For Leo, "To be under the authority of Peter was simply to be under the authority of Christ, and to repudiate the authority of Peter was to put oneself outside the mystery of the Church. For Leo, the coming of Peter to the centre of empire had been a providential act, designed so that from Rome the Gospel might spread to all the world" (Duffy, 43).

---

formal approbation, moral support, and advice. He also may have had a more particular motive, which may explain why he chose this particular time for his visit. Up until that point, Patrick hadn't established a central seat of the church in Ireland, no primatial or "metropolitan" church, for the chief bishop. But not long after his return, he founded the church of Armagh, fixing his own see there, and establishing it as the primatial church. This was an important step in the progress of ecclesiastical organization, and it is not a daring conjecture to suppose that Patrick wished to consult the Roman bishop concerning this design and obtain his approval.

The result of Patrick's visit to Rome is stated briefly in words that are probably a contemporary record: "He was approved in the Catholic faith." He may well have received practical advice from Pope Leo—such advice as a later pontiff gave to Augustine for the conversion of the English. Patrick also then carried back with him to Ireland visible and material proofs of the goodwill of Rome. He received gifts that, to Christians of his day, seemed to be the most precious of all possible gifts: relics of the greatest martyrs of all, the apostles Peter and Paul. A ridiculous story was later invented by medieval Irish clerics, anxious to justify a connection between Patrick and the medieval cult of the saints, that Patrick had thrown all of the inhabitants of Rome into a miraculous sleep, and then plundered the city of its most precious relics. But still, he apparently returned with opportune gifts for bestowing prestige upon the new church that he was about to found, and where they would afterwards be preserved.

CHAPTER THIRTEEN

The Preeminence of Armagh

No act of Patrick had more decisive consequences for the ecclesiastical history of the island than the foundation, soon after his return from Rome, of the church and monastery of Ardd Mache in the kingdom of Oriel. King Daire, through whose goodwill this community was established, dwelled in the neighborhood of the ancient fortress of Emain, which his own ancestors had destroyed a hundred years earlier when they came from the south to wrest the land from the Ulidians and sack the palace of its lords. The conquerors didn't set up their own abode in the stronghold of the old kings of Ulster; they burned the timber buildings and left the place desolate, as if it were under a curse. The ample earth structures of this royal stronghold are still there, attesting that Emain, famous in legend, was a place of historical importance in the days when Ulster belonged to one of the older tribes of the island. Long after the days of St. Patrick, the Picts made fruitless attempts, from their home in Dalaradia, to recover their storied palace. But it was not destined to become a place of human habitation again until, more than a thousand years after its desolation, a house was built there by an Ulster king "for the entertainment of the learned men of Ireland."

Patrick and King Daire

The house of King Daire was somewhere in the neighborhood. It seems possible that he was the king of Oriel, although

153

he may have only been the king of one of the tribes that belonged to the Oriel kingdom. Daire was not hostile towards Christianity, and he was easily persuaded to grant Patrick a site for a monastic foundation not far from his own dwelling.

Eastward from Emain, concealed from the eye by two high ridges, rises the hill known as Ardd Mache, "the height of Macha"—bearing the name of some heroine of legend. At the eastern foot of this hill, Daire apportioned a small tract of ground to Patrick, and this was the beginning of what was to become the chief ecclesiastical city of Ireland.

The simple houses that were needed for a small society of monks were built, and there is a record which appears to be ancient and credible about these buildings. A circular space was marked out, 140 feet in diameter and enclosed by a rampart of earth. Within this *less*, as it was called, a great house of wood was erected as the dwelling of the monks, with a kitchen and a small oratory. The dimensions of these houses are given as "27 feet in the Great House, 17 feet in the kitchen, 7 feet in the oratory; and this is how he always used to build the *congbala* (sacred enclosures)." This record has an interest beyond this particular monastery, as we may believe that it represents the typical scheme of the monastic establishments of Patrick and his companions. If these houses were circular, the numbers represent the diameters.

We don't know how long Patrick and his household lived under the hill of Macha, but the settlement was also not final. It seems that the bishop ultimately won great influence over the king, who evidently embraced the Christian faith, and then Daire resolved that the monastery should be raised from its lowly place to a loftier and safer site. A curious story, with the marks of antiquity about it, shows how all of this occurred. It would be difficult to say how much is fable and how much is underlying fact. The tale relates that Patrick had cast his eyes on the hill of Macha from the very beginning of his mission in Ireland. But Daire refused to grant it, and gave Patrick instead the land below. One day a squire of the king drove a horse to feed in a field of grass that belonged to the monastery. Patrick protested, but the squire did not answer, and when he returned to the field to fetch his horse the following day, it was dead. He told his master that the Christian had killed the beast, and Daire said to his men, "Go and kill him." But as the men were traveling there, an illness suddenly fell on Daire and his wife said, "It is the Christian who made this happen. Someone must go quickly and let his blessing be brought to us, and then my husband will be well. Tell those who went to slay him to stop!" At this, two men went to Patrick and told him that Daire was ill, and asked him for a remedy. Patrick gave them some water which he had consecrated. The men first sprinkled some of this water on the horse, and it was restored to life, and then, returning to Daire's house, they found it no less potent in restoring their lord to health.

Whatever may be thought of the anecdotes of the horse and the holy water, the story continues in very plausible fashion, showing that Patrick won the respect of Daire as a man of firm character. When all was done with the deaths and illness and restoration to life and health, Daire visited the monastery to pay respect to Patrick, and he offered him a large bronze vessel, a gift that he had imported from abroad. The bishop acknowledged the gift by saying, "I thank you," in Latin. The king was annoyed at this response, looking for some more elaborate and impressive acknowledgement. Patrick apparently spoke the Latin phrase, *gratias agamus* ("I thank you"), rapidly, and it sounded phonetically like *gratzacham*, or as meaningless gibberish. Upon returning home, Daire sent his servants to bring back the bronze, convinced that it was a thing that the Christian was unable to properly appreciate. When they returned with the vessel, Daire asked them what Patrick had said. "He said gratzacham," they told him. "What?" Daire resounded. "Gratzacham when it was given and gratzacham when it was taken away! It is a firm word, and for his gratzacham he shall have his cauldron." Then Daire went himself with the cauldron to Patrick and said, "Keep the cauldron, for you are a steadfast and unchangeable man." And he gave him the land that he desired, as well.

Daire granted Patrick the higher site, the land up on the hill, in honor of the bishop's character. So it came about that Patrick and his household went up from their home at the foot of the hill and made another home on its summit. The new settlement was probably constructed on the same plan, although it may have been slightly larger, to suit the area of the hilltop. The old settlement below may have been turned into a graveyard, and in later days a cloister was to arise there, known as the Temple of the Graveyard.

The Choice of Armagh

So it was, according to ancient tradition, that Armagh was founded. It soon rose to become the supreme ecclesiastical city in Ireland. Although we have no record of Patrick's own views, he seems to have consciously and deliberately laid the foundations of this preeminence. It is true that some of his successors in the see supported and enhanced its claim to supremacy and domination through misrepresentations and forgeries, just as in a larger sphere the later bishops of Rome sometimes made use of fabricated documents and accepted falsifications of history in order to establish their extravagant pretensions. But as in the case of Rome, misrepresentation of history at Armagh could only increase or confirm an authority that was already acknowledged, extending the limits of a power that had otherwise been established. If the church of Armagh had been originally on the same footing as any of the other churches that were founded by Patrick, it is inconceivable that it could have acquired the preeminence that it enjoyed by the seventh century.

We do not know of any political circumstances or historical events between the age of Patrick and the seventh century that would have served to elevate the church of Armagh above the churches of northern Ireland and invest it with an authority and prestige that did not originally belong to it. The only tenable explanation of the commanding position that Armagh occupied is that the tradition is substantially true, and that Patrick made this foundation near the derelict palace of the ancient Ulster kings. It is there that he made his own special seat and residence, and it was there that he exercised, and intended that his successors should exercise, an authority in Ireland that is similar to that of a metropolitan bishop in a province on the continent.

The choice of Armagh may seem strange. The hill of Macha was hardly a well-chosen spot as an ecclesiastical center. We might have expected him to seek a site somewhere in the kingdom of Meath, somewhere less distant from the hill of Uisnech, which the islanders regarded as the navel of their country. Or Trim, for instance, would have seemed to be a far more suitable seat for a bishop whose duties of supervision extended to Desmond as much as to Dalriada. But consider two points.

First, if we confine our view to the sphere of Patrick's own missionary activity, namely, northern Ireland, Armagh was a sufficiently convenient center. Meath and Connaught and the kingdoms of Ulster were the lands in which Patrick had chiefly worked, and they might have seemed to require closer supervision. Also, it may have been a matter of policy not to attempt to press his authority too strictly over the churches of the south. We will see next that though he visited southern Ireland, his work there was relatively slight.

The evidence suggests that while the whole island formed a single ecclesiastical province, in which Patrick occupied the position of bishop, there was actually—although not officially—a province within a province. He exerted a more direct and minute control over the northern part of the island. The position of a province cannot be entirely determined by a compass; geographical convenience cannot always be decisive.

Second, the fact that King Laoghaire was not a Christian may have weighed with Patrick against choosing a place in Meath. He may have thought it expedient to fix the chief seat of ecclesiastical authority in the territory and near the palace of a Christian king. If Daire was king of Oriel, his conversion to Christianity helps to explain the choice of Armagh, in contrast to the obduracy of Laoghaire. A secure position near the gates of a powerful king would have counted for much, and his conversion would have been the greatest single triumph that Patrick had yet achieved.

Our oldest records don't describe Patrick's work in the kingdoms of Ulster with the same details or at the same length as his work in Connaught. But they indicate that he preached and founded churches in the kingdoms of Ailech and Oriel, as well as in Ulidia. And there is reason to believe that fuller records once existed, which were used by one of the earlier biographers.

Travel in the South, and Church Discipline

While Patrick's sphere of immediate activity seems to have been mainly in the northern half of the island, there is not much room for serious doubts that he claimed to hold authority over the southern provinces as well. His own description of himself not as bishop in a particular province, but as bishop in Ireland generally, is sufficient to make this clear. And there are various records of his visits to Leinster and Munster.

Patrick probably baptized the sons of Dunlang, king of Leinster, and he is recorded to have visited the royal palace at the hill of Cashel and baptized the sons of Natfraich, king of Munster. He was remembered to have passed through Ossory, and worked in the regions of Muskerry. If Christianity made greater strides in the southern kingdoms, he had less to do as a pioneer, but just as much to do as an organizer. Scanty are the records of his work in the south, but this may be because of his special association with the see of Armagh.

In Leinster, Patrick had two fellow workers, Auxilius and Iserninus, whom he had known at Auxerre. They had been sent to Ireland about six years after Patrick's own coming. The origin of Auxilius is unknown. His name is still commemorated by a church that he founded not far from Naas. Iserninus was of Irish birth; his native name was Fith, and he was born in the neighborhood of Clonmore on the borders of Carlow and Wicklow. It was there that he first set up a church, but his ultimate establishment was at Aghade, on the River Slaney. All of these regions formed part of a considerable kingdom that was at this time ruled over by Endae Cennsalach. This king opposed the diffusion of the new faith, and Iserninus found it prudent to withdraw beyond the borders of his kingdom. Perhaps he found a refuge at Old Kilcullen in what is now County Kildare—one of the strongholds of the kings of Leinster. But eventually Crimthann, the son and successor of Endae, was converted and baptized by Patrick at his dwelling on the banks of the Slaney, where earthworks still mark a seat of the kings of Cennsalach's successors.

This case is similar to that of the sons of Amolngaid, and illustrates the general fact that while the older generation was still fervently clinging to the old beliefs, the younger generation was steadily turning to the new. The conversion of Crimthann enabled Iserninus to return to his own land and he established himself at Aghade, a crossing place on the Slaney about nine miles below Rathvilly.

Among the actions ascribed to Patrick in Leinster, the consecration of Fiacc the Fair, a pupil of the poet Dubthach, deserves mention. Fiacc was converted into a Christian bishop, according to tradition, and there seems to be little reason to doubt it. Patrick gave him a bell, a staff, a writing tablet, and the cup and paten used for the Eucharist. These things are still preserved. Fiacc settled first at a church not far from Tallow, but he afterwards became bishop of Slebte, on the western bank of the River Barrow, and ended his days there. In the early Middle Ages, Slebte was a notable place on the ecclesiastical map, but the desolate site shows no vestiges of its ancient importance. At the end of the seventh century, Slebte renewed the ties that bound it to Armagh in the days of Fiacc and Patrick, and we possess a monument of this reconciliation in the earliest biography of Patrick, the *Life* by Muirchu, who was a clerk of Fiacc's church.

It is unclear whether Auxilius and Iserninus were already invested as bishops when they left Gaul for Ireland, or if they were consecrated in Leinster by Patrick. But in any case, together with Seachnaill, who came with them from Gaul, they held an exceptional position of weight as counselors. They may have come from the episcopal city where Patrick himself had been trained, corroborating the Gallic influence of Auxerre that presided at the organization of the church in Ireland.

Consecrating Bishops

Scholars cannot agree about how many bishops Patrick may have consecrated. Some say as many as 450. Perhaps Patrick consecrated entire clans of converted religious leaders as bishops? Other scholars say that 150 is a more likely number. But still others argue that Patrick couldn't have consecrated a single bishop, since he was the only bishop in Ireland during his era and it is supposed to take three bishops to lay hands on another (Hood, 14).

Patrick took special counsel with these men for laying down rules of ecclesiastical discipline, and on one occasion a body of rules was drawn up in the form of a circular letter addressed by Patrick, Auxilius, and Iserninus to all the clergy of Ireland. The miscellaneous regulations are arranged in a haphazard manner and were evidently prompted by abuses or practical difficulties that had come to the notice of the framers. They mostly deal with the discipline of the clergy. They testify to such irregularities as a bishop interfering in his neighbor's diocese, vagabond clerks going from place to place, churches founded without permission of the bishop. It was ordained that no cleric from Britain shall minister in Ireland unless he has brought a letter from his superior. All the clergy, from the priest to the doorkeeper, are to wear the complete Roman tonsure, and their wives are to veil their heads. A monk and a consecrated virgin are not to drive from house to house in the same carriage, or indulge in protracted conversations. Provision was also made for stringent enforcement of sentences of excommunication.

One of the most important duties of Irish Christians at this time was the redemption of Christian captives from slavery. However, this goal and activity furnished an easy opportunity for some to practice deception. A rule was drawn up in this same circular letter which provided that no one shall privately and without permission take a collection of money, and that, if there is ever a surplus from a collection, it shall be placed on the altar of the church and kept for a later need. It is interesting to note that they also drew up a prohibition against accepting alms from pagans. This points to the comprehensive religious view of some, perhaps many, of the still unconverted; Laoghaire himself may have been an instance—who, although not prepared to abandon their own cults, were ready to pay some homage to the new deity whose reality and power they couldn't question.

In a church growing up in a heathen land, the bishops seem to have found it inexpedient and impracticable to enforce long periods of penitence for transgressions we would normally regard more seriously than they once were. In fact, some of these transgressions were apparently regarded more lightly in Ireland than in the Roman Empire at this time. We find that only a year of penance was imposed on those who committed manslaughter or fornication, or on those who are shown to consult a soothsayer; and only half a year for an act of theft.

CHAPTER FOURTEEN
Cloisters and Chieftains

In his *Confession*, St. Patrick describes some of the features of his work in Ireland. He created an ecclesiastical organization, chose and ordained clergy, for a people that had been recently turning to the Christian faith. He also repeatedly insists that he planted that faith in regions that were wholly heathen, in the extreme parts of the island. He spread his nets so that a large multitude "might be caught for God," and so that there might be clergy everywhere to baptize and encourage people needing and craving their service. He says that he baptized thousands, and this doesn't need to be considered hyperbole, and ordained ministers everywhere. The foundation of monastic communities is understood by his incidental observation that young natives have become monks, and daughters of chieftains, "virgins of Christ." These maidens, he says, generally took their vows against the will of their fathers and were ready to suffer persecution from their parents. He mentions especially a beautiful woman of noble birth whom he baptized. A few days after the ceremony she came to him and intimated that she had received a direct warning from God that she should become a "virgin of Christ." Her parents appear to have also embraced Christianity by this time; however, they had a natural repugnance to seeing their children withdrawn from the claims of the family and the world. The ultimate triumph on which Patrick dwells in this passage is not the triumph of Christian faith, but of the monastic ideal.

Patrick refers to perils that he had to pass through in his work. He says that divine aid "delivered me often from bondage and from twelve dangers by which my life was endangered." On one occasion, he and his companions were seized and his captors wished to kill him. His belongings were taken from him and he was kept in chains for two weeks, until, through the intervention of influential friends, he was set free and his property restored. Experiences such as these would probably have been more common if Patrick had not used a policy that worked well for him: he used to purchase the goodwill and protection of the kings by giving them presents. In the same way he provided for the security of the clergy in those districts that he most frequently visited, by paying large sums to the judges and local leaders. Patrick claims to have distributed among the judges at least "the value of fifteen men." All of these expenses were defrayed from his own purse. We may ask the obvious questions: Where did Patrick get this money? Did he inherit from his father? But we don't know the answers.

Another feature of his policy, on which Patrick prided himself, was dealing plainly and sincerely with the Irish. He never went back on his word, and he never resorted to tricks in order to win some advantage for "God and the Church." He believed that by adhering strictly to this policy of straightforwardness he averted persecutions.

While Patrick was assisted by many foreign fellow workers, it was his aim to create a native clergy. And it was a matter of high importance to find likely youths and educate them for church work. Our records illustrate this amply. Benignus, who afterwards succeeded Patrick in Armagh, was said to have been adopted by him as a young boy soon after coming to Ireland. Sachall, who accompanied Patrick to Rome, was another instance. A similar policy was contemplated by Pope Gregory the Great for England. We have a letter that he wrote to a presbyter, bidding him to purchase in Gaul English boy slaves of seventeen and eighteen years of age, for the purpose of educating them in monasteries.

Monastery and Tribe

The churches and cloisters that were founded by Patrick and his companions seem, in most cases, to have been established on land that was devoted to the purpose by chieftains or nobles from their own private property. The interests of the tribe, and the interests of the proprietor's, or the chieftain's, descendants, had to be considered. We find that in some cases the proprietor did not make over all his rights to the church community, but retained them and transmitted to his descendants a certain control over it. This local control was then shared by the family side-by-side with the abbot, or spiritual head of the new community. There were thus two lines of succession—the secular one, in which the descent was hereditary, and the ecclesiastical one, which was sometimes regularly connected by blood with the founder. This dual system kept the church or monastery in close touch with the tribe.

In other cases, the connection of the monastery with the tribe was secured by establishing a family right of inheritance to the position of abbot. There was only a spiritual succession; the undivided authority lay with the abbot, but the abbots could be chosen only from the founder's family. Such a provision might be made conditionally or unconditionally. The monastery of Drumlease in Leitrim, which was founded by Fethfio, furnishes an example of the former. Fethfio laid down that the inheritance to Drumlease should not be confined unconditionally to his own family. His family should inherit the succession, if there was any member pious and good and conscientious. But if not, the abbot should be chosen from the community or monks of Drumlease.

But in other cases the original proprietor seems to have alienated his land and placed it entirely in the hands of an ecclesiastical founder, who was either a member of another tribe or a foreigner. But the tribe within whose territory the land lay had a word to say. It seems to have been a general rule that the privilege of succession belonged to the founder's tribe, but that if no suitable successor could be found in that tribe, the abbacy should pass to the tribe within whose territory the monastery stood.

In the earliest records, we find other foundations that are expressly distinguished as "free." This seems to imply a release from restrictions and obligations that were usually imposed, and a greater measure of independence of the tribe. Thus, in Sligo a large district was offered by its owners and the king, who "made it free to God and Patrick."

The church in the Roman Empire has been described as an *imperium in imperio*, "an order within an order," and the typical ecclesiastical community in Ireland may be described as a tribe within a tribe. The abbot, or where the dual system prevailed, his lay coadjutor, exercised power over the people of the surrounding community just as a tribal king exercised power over the tribe. The community, even though it was constituted as a separate body and formed a tribe by itself, was nevertheless bound by certain obligations to the tribe within whose borders it lay. In general, the monastery was bound to furnish religious services required by the tribe, but also to rear and educate without cost the offspring of any tribesman who chose to devote his son to a religious life. The tribesman was bound not to withdraw his child, once the child had been consigned to the care of the monks, without paying a penalty.

We should also note that the member of a religious house, although he belonged to a society that managed its affairs separately from a tribe, did not altogether cease to be a tribesman. If he was murdered, for instance, compensation (from the murderer's family) was due not to the monastery but to the tribe. Upon his father's death, he inherited his portion of the family property, just as any of his brothers would, but we cannot say how far, in early times, the tribe permitted a monastic community to exercise rights over land that was inherited by one of its members. In

Imperium

Bury's allusion to the Latin word *imperium* is well-chosen. Perhaps no other word tells the story of the conflicts of the Roman Church with the civil authorities better than this one. This word, which literally means "power," is used throughout medieval history in disputes between church and state. There are many examples, but here are two: Pope Gregory IX (1227–1241), during the days immediately after St. Francis of Assisi, declared for himself *imperium animarum,* "command of the souls," in contrast to the secular authority of Emperor Frederick II. The Church of England was created when King Henry VIII's parliament declared that the Roman Catholic Church's policy of *imperio in imperio,* "state in the state" was no longer valid. It was then that the sovereign of England became known as the "head" of the Church in England.

later times, the church assumed possession, allowing the monk to hold his inheritance as a tenant, and furnishing him with stock. But this custom may not have been introduced until the church had waxed in power and cupidity. It is also uncertain what claims the newborn monasteries may have pressed, in their early years, on the liberality of those who had permitted their foundation. At some point after Patrick's day, they claimed not only firstfruits and tithes and the firstlings of animals, but also firstborn sons. And when a man had ten sons, the monastery claimed another, as well as the eldest. These audacious claims were modeled on the law of Moses, but we don't know how far they were actually pressed. It is certain, however, that rights of this kind were not and could not have been sought by Patrick and his contemporaries.

Not all of Patrick's ecclesiastical foundations took the shape of monastic societies, however. Many of the churches he founded were served by only one or two clerics, and furnished with only enough land to support them. Still, the monastic foundations were a prominent feature of the overall organization of the church in Ireland. They were centers for propagating Christianity and schools for educating the clergy. They also served the religious needs of the immediate district. A staff of clergy was attached, and the abbot was frequently also a bishop.

Irish Independence

The need for this sort of monastic organization was surely due to the fact that there were no cities in Ireland. Centers had to be created for church purposes, and it was almost a matter of course that these church towns would be constructed on the monastic principle. If towns had existed, they would have been the ecclesiastical centers, the seats of the bishops, and the bishops wouldn't have been abbots or attached to monasteries. The fact that the Latin word *civitas*, "city," was used to designate these religious/secular communities illustrates the motive of this singular organization.

At the same time, Patrick consecrated bishops with definite and distinct sees, or jurisdictions. The maintenance of the diocesan structure, in Patrick's day, must have been controlled from above. He would have exercised this higher authority himself, and probably attached it to the see that he occupied, the see of Armagh. We know that this diocesan organization, in the course of the subsequent development of religious institutions, largely broke down, for various reasons. The ecclesiastical communities of Ireland were animated by the same impulse to independence as the tribes—and it was difficult for the bishop of Armagh, as for the king of Ireland, to exert effectual authority. The independent tribal spirit was not flexible or readily obedient to the distant control of a prelate who was a member of another tribe. There was no secular power able or willing to enforce submission to the higher jurisdiction. Thus, it was a continual struggle for the bishops of Armagh to maintain the position that Patrick had bequeathed to them. During the sixth century, new and powerful monastic communities arose within their province, outstripping the original churches in zeal, learning, and reputation. It was not until the end of the seventh century that the church of Armagh began to succeed in reestablishing its power and ecclesiastical unity. But at no time were the church people of Ireland more conspicuous and famous in other lands for learning and piety than in the sixth and seventh centuries.

After Patrick's death, his work was partly undone, and the Irish Church developed on lines that were quite different from his original design. Irish monks abandoned the recognized mode of shaving the head that he had enjoined, and adopted the native tonsure of the Druids. The central authority of Armagh couldn't maintain itself against the centrifugal spirit of the land or resist the love of local independence that operated in all affairs. Monasticism—an institution that appears to have been intensely attractive to the temper of the people—ran riot, we might say, at the expense of ecclesiastical organization. Abbots became more important than bishops. The political changes in Gaul and Italy, connected with the dismemberment of the empire, tended to keep Ireland out of touch with the continental churches in the latter part of the fifth and in the sixth century. The injunction to appeal to Rome, although no one would have thought of repudiating it, was a dead letter. Looking at Irish Christianity as it appears in the seventh century, when the movement set out to bring it into line with the rest of the Western Church, leads many to assume that Patrick inaugurated the peculiar features that were really alien to the spirit of his work. Whatever concessions and modifications he may have found it necessary or political to make, he certainly didn't anticipate or intend the developments that actually ensued.

But even though his organization partially collapsed, and even though the Irish Christians didn't live up to his ideal of the *unitas ecclesiae*, there was one feature of his policy that was never undone: he made Latin the spiritual language of Ireland. The people of Ireland used to remember that Patrick would write alphabets for young people who had been chosen for a priestly career—this was the first step in teaching them Latin, the language of the church universal.

There must have been some knowledge of the Latin alphabet in Ireland before Patrick. It was clearly not an entirely new thing when he arrived, but his work seems to have secured it a new position. We cannot say for certain whether the introduction of the Latin script originated a written Irish literature, or if it only displaced an older form of writing in which literature already existed. In the mist that rests over the early history of Ireland, this is one of the darkest points. It would be out of place to discuss the matter too much here, but one or two considerations may be briefly noted.

The mode of writing possessed by the early Irish—although how much earlier than the fifth century we don't know for sure—seems to have been mainly used for engraving names on tombstones. And it was alphabetic. The characters, which were called ogams, consisted of strokes and points, probably a native invention, since such inscriptions are found only in Ireland and in regions of the British Isles that came within the range of Irish influence. But the alphabet itself was not a native invention; it is simply the Latin alphabet—*a b c d e f g h i l m n o p q r s t u v*, and *ng* (a guttural nasal, as occurs in the name Amolngaid)—with the last three letters left out, a new letter added, and with *u* differentiated into two letters, representing its two sounds. We don't have any evidence that the Irish ever employed, besides their monumental script, another system of symbols suitable for literature and the business of life, other than this, the Roman. The absence of evidence, however, is not decisive. We should remember that writing was in use among the Celtic Iberians of Spain and the Celts of Gaul before the Roman conquest (AD 43). The Iberians had their own script, and some of the Spanish peoples had a considerable literature. In Gaul, we are told by Caesar that the lore of the Druids wasn't written down, but that Greek writing was used for public and private purposes. This means that the Gallic tongue was written in Greek characters, and some examples of such writing have been preserved. These facts show, at least, that the art of writing might have reached Ireland at an early period. But there is no proof that it did. If any pre-Roman alphabet was ever used, it has left no traces of its presence. But the Roman, Latin, alphabet was introduced at some point after the Roman occupation of Britain. And from it some learned person in Ireland constructed the ogam cipher for sepulchral uses. The diffusion of Christianity tended to diffuse the use of writing, but Latin letters were a gift that the pagans of Ireland received from the empire, independently of the gift of Christianity.

St. Martin of Tours

Bury never mentions the legend that Patrick was related, on his mother's side, to Martin of Tours. Today, most scholars do not take this legend seriously, but Martin's life and work did have some influence on Patrick's development. The first *Life* of Martin was written within two decades of the saint's death in 397, and was read widely during Patrick's day.

Martin was a soldier for the Roman Empire in his teens, and he famously cut his elegant military cloak down the middle, to give half to a beggar. Soon after this incident, Martin became one of the first Christian pacifists, declaring to his superior,

"I am a soldier of Christ. I can no longer fight." He later became the bishop of Tours, in southern France, and established the first monastic houses in western Europe during the middle of the fourth century. Patrick's own education at Lerins would have been infused with the teachings and legendary influence of the earlier Martin. Martin was known for the fervor with which he destroyed pagan temples in western France, and for combating Druidic religious practices. His tomb in Tours is a stopping point on the pilgrimage route to Santiago de Compostela in northwestern Spain.

CHAPTER FIFTEEN

His Denunciation of Coroticus, *and the* Confession

Christianity was introduced among the Picts of Galloway at the beginning of the fifth century by a Briton who is little more than a name. Ninian, educated at Rome, had probably come under the influence of St. Martin of Tours. He then devoted himself to the task of preaching his faith in the wilds of Galloway, where, on the inner promontory that runs out towards the Isle of Man, he built a stone church. As the only stone building in this uncivilized land, it became known as the White House. An important monastic establishment grew around it, which enjoyed a high reputation in Ireland in the sixth century, and was known there as the Great Monastery.

The work of St. Ninian was like the work of his contemporary Victricius in Gaul, being missionary work within the Roman Empire—that is, if Galloway and its inhabitants belonged to the Roman province of Valentia. After the Roman legions were withdrawn from Britain and the island was cut off from the central control of the empire, the task of maintaining order in the western part of the province of Valentia seems to have been undertaken by one of those rulers who sprang up in various parts of the island. These rulers were variously styled as "kings" or "tyrants."

A word must be said about the condition of Britain in the fifth century, because it is generally misunderstood. It is wrong to assume that the withdrawal of the Roman legions from Britain in 407, and the mandate of the Emperor Honorius three or four years later permitting the citizens of Britain to arm themselves and provide for their own defense, meant the instant departure of all things Roman from British shores. Roman traditions and civilization carried on. The idea that the island almost immediately relapsed into something resembling its pre-Roman condition is due partly to the scanty nature of our evidence. It is also due to a misreading of the famous work of Gildas the Wise (ca. 490s–ca. 570) "on the decline and fall of Britain," to a mistaken idea of the isolation of Britain from the continent, and to that anachronistic habit of judging a man's acts and thoughts as if they could have foreseen the future. No one would have thought, in those early days, that the dismemberment of the empire had cut Britain off forever. The empire had weathered storms before and emerged stable and strong; to the contemporaries of Honorius and Valentinian the empire was part of the established order of things, and a suspension of its control in any particular portion of its dominion was something temporary and passing. The British provincials still considered themselves part of the empire. For at least 150 years after 407, some of them considered themselves Roman citizens.

The traditions and machinery of the Roman administration would not have immediately disappeared the moment that the central authorities ceased to control it. What could the provincials have put in its place? There was doubtless a Celtic revival, but for many years after the mandate of Honorius, Roman institutions must have continued to exist alongside, or to be controlled by, the local authorities, those "kings" and "tyrants." The man whom we find in the reign of Valentinian III, ruling in Strathclyde, maintaining such law and order as might be maintained, was named Coroticus.

Coroticus founded a line of kings who were still reigning at the end of the following century. His seat was the Rock of Clyde. As the seat of a British ruler, amid surrounding Scots and Picts, this stronghold came to be known as "the fort of the Britons," which was corrupted into the modern Dumbarton. His power was maintained by soldiers and his position is distinct from that of pre-Roman chiefs of British tribes. His soldiers may actually have been the successors of the Roman troops who had defended the north. His position—whether he assumed any Roman military title or not—may be compared to that of the general Aegidius, who maintained the name of the empire in north Gaul when it had been cut off from the rest of the empire. Aegidius transmitted his authority to his son Syagrius, as Coroticus transmitted his to his son Cinuit; and if Syagrius hadn't been overthrown by the Franks, a state would have been formed in Belgica that would have resembled in origin the state that Coroticus formed in Strathclyde. Of course the Gallo-Roman generals were in touch with the empire, maintained the imperial machinery, and had a position different from the irregular position of the semi-barbarous Briton on his rock by the Clyde. But we may be sure that Coroticus was careful to make the most of his claim to represent the imperial tradition and rule over Roman citizens.

Coroticus was the ruler of Strathclyde in the days of Patrick. We can easily imagine that he may have sometimes found it difficult to pay his soldiers and retainers, and that for this purpose he may have been forced to plunder his neighbors. In any case, we know that he fitted out a marauding expedition; it doesn't appear that he led it himself, but it crossed the channel and descended on the coast of Ireland, probably in Dalaradia. Perhaps it was a reprisal for raids that the Scots and Picts of these lands may have made on his dominion. Or it may have been, for all we know, an episode in a regular war. In any event, he was supported in this enterprise by the Picts of Galloway, who had relapsed into heathenism, and by some of those heathen Scots who had come over from Ireland and settled in the region northwest of the Clyde.

In the course of their devastation these heathen allies of Coroticus appeared on the scene of a Christian ceremony. Neophytes, who had just been baptized and anointed with the baptismal chrism, were standing in white raiment. The sign of the cross was still fragrant on their foreheads when the heathen rushed upon them, put some to the sword, and carried others away captive. Whether or not he was there in person, Patrick must have been near the spot of the outrage, for he was informed of it so soon that on the next day he dispatched one of his most trusted priests, one whom he had trained from childhood, to the soldiers of Coroticus. The emissary requested that the captives be released and the booty returned. The message, which must have reached them before they left Ireland, was received with mockery, although the soldiers of Coroticus were Christians and "Romans," and it was not they but their heathen allies who had massacred the defenseless Christians.

It is not clear whether Coroticus himself was present when the message was delivered, but it is certain that Patrick regarded him as responsible. We may suppose that Coroticus had declined to interfere before Patrick wrote the letter. And the letter is our only record of this event. The only thing that the indignant bishop could do for the release of his "sons and daughters" was to bring the public opinion of the Christians in Strathclyde to bear upon Coroticus and his soldiers. He wrote a strong letter, addressing it, apparently, to the general Christian community in the dominion of Coroticus, and requiring them to have no dealings with the guilty "tyrant" and his soldiers: "not to take food or drink with them, not to receive alms from them, nor show respect to them, until they should repent in tears and make satisfaction to God by releasing the Christian captives."

Patrick asked that his letter be read before all the people in the presence of Coroticus. Guilt for the outrage was laid entirely upon Coroticus; it was ascribed to the orders he gave. He was called a betrayer of Christians into the hands of Scots and Picts. Patrick wrote, "It is the custom of Roman Christians in Gaul to send good men to the Franks and other heathens to redeem captives for so many thousand pieces of gold. You, on the contrary, murder Christians and sell them to a foreign nation that doesn't know God. You deliver members of Christ, as it were, into a house of ill repute."

The sequel to this episode is unknown. We have no records to tell us if the letter of Patrick had any effect on the obstinate hearts of Coroticus and his soldiers, or whether the clergy to whom it was addressed applied the pressure of excommunication—which Patrick begged them to put in force. But this letter holds interest for the biographer beyond the details of the occurrence that provoked it. Besides the wrathful indignation that animates Patrick's language, there is also a strain of bitterness that reveals another motive. He was clearly afraid that his message would not be received with friendship or sympathy by the British Christians to whom it is sent. He complained expressly that his work in Ireland was regarded in Britain (his own country) with envy and a lack of charity. He wrote, "If my own do not know me—well, 'a prophet has no honor in his own country.' We don't belong to one sheepfold, nor do we have one God for our father." He referred to his own biography, to his birth as a Roman citizen, to his unselfish

Impolite Patrick

"We can be reasonably sure . . . that the letter [to Coroticus] infuriated the leaders of the British church. Early church documents state repeatedly that priests and bishops should not interfere with the congregation of other bishops. Church tradition demanded that Patrick contact the bishop of the British town where Coroticus lived and ask him to discipline the wayward tyrant himself." (Freeman, 140)

motives in undertaking the toil of a preacher of the Gospel in a barbarous land where he lived as a stranger and exile, as if he had to justify himself against the envy and injustice of jealous detractors. "I am envied." "Some despise me." We must note this tone of bitterness in the letter, as it almost suggests that, in Patrick's opinion, the envy and dislike he felt was partly responsible for the outrage itself.

There is no extant evidence to fix the date of this episode, but the dominance of the same bitter note in the other extant writing of Patrick, written in the author's old age, makes it probable that the letter belongs to the later rather than to the earlier period of his labors in Ireland.

His Confession, Literacy, and Detractors

People of action who help to change the face of the world by impressing upon it ideas that others have originated seldom have the time or inclination to record their work in writing. The great apostles of Europe illustrate this fact. None of them, from Wulfilas to Otto of Bamberg (German missionary to Pomerania—the regions of west Germany and east Poland—d. 1139), has left a relation of his own apostolic labors. We are lucky if a disciple took thought for posterity to write a brief narrative of his master's actions. But although neither Patrick nor any of the other apostles who preached to the Celts, Germans, or Slavs wrote the story of his own life, some of them have left literary records that bear on their work. Fortunately, in Patrick's case, circumstances occasionally forced him to write.

The *Confession* is of far greater interest and value than the *Letter Against Coroticus*. Although it is not an autobiography, it contains highly important autobiographical passages; we've made reference to many of them already in these pages. It was written in Patrick's old age, at a time when he felt that death might not be very far off. He said, "This is my confession before I die." The title of *Confession*, however, may easily convey a false idea. The writer has occasion to confess certain sins, he has occasion also to make a brief confession of the articles of his faith, but it is in neither of these senses that he calls the work as a whole his confession. Neither his sins nor his theological creed are his main theme, but the wonderful ways of God in dealing with his own life. "I must not hide the gift of God"— this is what he "confesses"; this is the refrain that pervades the *Confession* and emphatically marks its purpose.

The text says nothing of miracles, in the sense of violations of natural laws. Patrick's own strange life seemed to him to be more marvelous than any miracle in that special meaning of the word. The *Confession* reveals vividly his intense wondering consciousness at the great work that had fallen just to him, out of the multitude of all others, to carry out a great work to extend the borders of Christendom. As he looked back on his past life, it seemed unutterably strange that the careless boy in the British town had shone as a light to the Gentiles, and the ways that this happened made it seem still more mysterious. But what impressed him above all as a divine miracle was that he felt the assurance of success at the outset. What we might describe as a person's overruling imperative desire, accompanied by a secret consciousness of his own capacity to attempt a difficult task, seemed to Patrick to be a direct revelation from one who had foreknowledge of the future. The express motive of the *Confession* is to declare the wonderful dealings of God with himself, as a sort of repayment or thanksgiving.

Did Patrick Know Augustine's *Confessions*?

Augustine of Hippo (AD 354–430) wrote his first-ever autobiography between 397–398, while in his early forties. Augustine's book is different in many ways from Patrick's. Augustine set out to actually confess his sins—of theft, lust, fornication, and pride—as well as the earlier, heretical beliefs that he held before his conversion to Catholicism. It is a narrative of his intellectual, spiritual, and physical life up until that point. Would Patrick have known it? Most likely, yes. Augustine was famous in the west since the age of thirty, in AD 384, when he was awarded a prominent academic position. By 396, he was the bishop of Hippo, in northern Africa, a post that he held for more than thirty years. He was famous by his death, and his writings were read in Latin by clergy throughout the western world.

It would hardly have been necessary to make such a declaration in writing if it hadn't seemed to him that his life and work were partly misunderstood. Inevitably, a man of Patrick's force of character and achievements would have aroused some feelings of jealousy and voices of detraction—and the *Confession* is evidently a reply to things that were said to belittle him. One charge that was brought against Patrick was his lack of literary education. His deficiency in this respect was probably spoken as a disqualification for the eminent position of authority he had won by his practical labors. Compared with most of the many bishops in Gaul, and perhaps with most of the few bishops in Britain, Patrick might have been described as illiterate. In the eyes of his countryman Faustus, or in the eyes of Sidonius Apollinaris, the bishop of Armagh would have seemed, so far as style is concerned, unworthy to hold a pen.

On this count, Patrick disarms the criticism by a full admission of his *rusticitas*, his lack of culture, and acknowledges that as he grows old he feels his deficiency more and more. This consciousness of literary incompetence had previously kept him from writing his reflections, but now he resolved to make things plain. He goes on to explain by passages from his life how he happened to take on the work of converting heathen people, despite missing the early training which is desirous in a religious apostle. His narrative is designed to show that it was entirely God's doing, who singled him out, untrained and unskilled though he was. He explained that there were no worldly inducements to support the divine command, that he obeyed simply without any ulterior motive, and in opposition to the wish of his family.

This all points to another imputation that stung him more than the true taunt of illiteracy. His detractors must have hinted that Patrick's motives for preaching to the Scots were not entirely pure. He doesn't conceal that the island in which he had toiled as a captive slave was without attraction for him; he implies that he always felt as a stranger there, a stranger in a strange land. "I testify," he says, summing up, "in truth and in exultation of heart, before God and His holy angels, that I never had any motive except for the gospel and the promises of God, to return at any time to those people from whom I had previously escaped."

He repudiates the implication that he won any personal profit in worldly goods from those whom he converted, or that he sought in any way to benefit from the people among whom he lived. To show how discreetly he ordered his ways, how careful he was in avoiding all scandalous suspicion, he mentions that when men and women of his flock sent him gifts, or laid ornaments on the altar, he always returned them at the risk of offending the givers.

Patrick's Money

"How was Patrick's mission financed? This is a problem that his own writings do not solve. He has refused gifts from pious women, and taken nothing for all his baptisms and confirmations. He says 'I have no wealth'; yet he has traveled everywhere dispensing generous patronage" (Croinin, 308).

It is easy to read between the lines the detractions that probably wounded St. Patrick, even if we'll never quite know whose voices he was hearing. There are some indications that it was from his own country and countrymen that the charges to which he obliquely refers were brought against him. At the end of the composition he says that he wrote it "in Ireland," and this gives us a reasonable ground for supposing that it was addressed mainly to people outside Ireland. When he speaks of "those people whom I live among," and when he mentions "women of our race" rather than women of *my* race, he is addressing some of his British fellow countrymen, not his Irish disciples. If this "apology" for his life had been meant first of all for Ireland, he would have taken some care to veil his feeling of homelessness. And he wouldn't have shown so clearly that he felt as an alien on foreign soil, and that he was abiding there only from a sense of duty, not from the longings of his heart. All of this is borne out by the writer's express statement that he wishes his "brothers and family" to know his character and nature.

Those who disparaged him were clearly some of the British fellow workers who had labored with him in propagating the Christian faith in Ireland. Jealousy and friction must have risen up between the chief apostle and some of his helpers; it may be that some of those who felt themselves aggrieved returned in disgust to Britain and indulged their ill feelings by spreading evil reports about Patrick's conduct of the Irish mission. The *Confession* was primarily intended for the communities in Britain where such reports were circulated; it was to refute those who set them afloat.

We know of one specific attack on Patrick that seems to have caused him more distress and agitation of spirit than any other experience during his work in Ireland. Before he was ordained a deacon, he had confessed to a trusted friend a fault that he had committed at the age of fifteen. His friend evidently didn't consider it an obstacle to ordination, and afterwards supported the proposal that Patrick should be consecrated bishop for Ireland. But later, he betrayed the secret, and the youthful indiscretion came to the ears of people whom we might identify with some of Patrick's foreign coadjutors. It is clear that the attack was made in Ireland, and they were probably ecclesiastics; they may have come from Britain for the purpose of attacking him. "They came," he says in his simple style, "and argued that my sins should prevent my laborious episcopate." These words demonstrate that he had already labored for some years—other indications suggest fifteen or sixteen years—when this attack was made. He doesn't tell us how he met or weathered the danger, and he ascribes his escape from stain and trouble to divine assistance.

The vision that Patrick saw the night after a conversation with the clerics remains ambiguous, for he tells it so badly.

"That night I saw in a vision of the night a writing that had been written against me, dishonoring me. And at the same time I heard the answer of God saying to me, 'We have seen with displeasure the face of' the person, revealing his name." We can sympathize with him in his deep resentment of an attack so manifestly unjust, of a friend's treachery so apparently inexcusable. But the incident shows that people existed who were distinctly hostile to him. His lack of culture had previously been the only reproach that they could offer; but when they discovered a moral delinquency, even though it was more than forty years old, the opportunity proved irresistible.

While his vindication was addressed to people beyond Ireland, it was also intended for the Irish. It might almost be described as an open letter to his brothers in Britain, published in Ireland. He describes it himself as "an offering to my brethren, and to my children whom I baptized," for the purpose of making known "the gift of God," *donum Dei*.

When Patrick Sinned

"Speculation has centered on what type of sin Patrick committed in his youth that could have blocked his elevation to the episcopate. Patrick does not tell us *what* sin it was, but he does tell us *when* the sin was committed: it was while he was in a state of 'death and unbelief,' that is, before he was baptized. . . . As baptism removes all sins, Patrick would have been pure at the time he was preparing for the diaconate, and hence the revelation of his youthful sin should have had no relevance to his ecclesiastical career. Secondly, we learn from the same passage that Patrick did not receive baptism as an infant even though his father was a deacon and his grandfather a priest." (Herren/Brown, 83–84)

The Real and the Mythic Patrick

The spirit and tone of the *Confession* are so consistently humble that it almost lends itself to a misperception. Were Patrick's achievements smaller, and the sphere of his work more restricted, than our other sources tell us? It has even been said that the *Confession* is a confession of a life's failure. Any such interpretation misreads the document entirely. On the

Confessional Patrick

R.P.C. Hanson, the most respected of recent biographers of Patrick, believes that the *Confession* and *Letter Against Coroticus* are the earliest examples of forthright, revealing, confessional writing. "One could almost go further than this and say that Patrick is the first British personality in history whom historians can know" (Hanson, 200).

contrary, the main argument is that the success Patrick had been led to hope and expect—through divine intimations, as he believed—had been brought to pass. Failure is never proven by the absence of boasts. The proud consciousness of the writer that his life had been fruitful and prosperous comes out more subtly in the implied comparison he suggests between himself and the first apostle of the Gentiles, by quotations and echoes from Paul's epistles. In fact, the Second Letter to the Corinthians seems to have been especially before him. This was natural; in it, Paul was vindicating his character.

We read how the exile would not visit Britain, his home, or Gaul, where he had many friends, because he felt himself bound by the spirit to spend the rest of his life in his chosen banishment. He desired to maintain his work and to protect by his influence the Christians who were in danger. His energy and perseverance had accomplished a great deal, and he decided not to desert it until death compelled him.

His two writings furnish the only evidence we have for forming an idea of his character. The other documents, on which we depend for the outline of his life and work, preserve genuine records of events, but reflect the picture of a man who mustn't be mistaken for the historical Patrick. The bishop of British birth and Roman education is gradually transformed into a typical Irish saint, dear to the popular imagination, who curses both people and inanimate things, as they incur his displeasure. He arranges with the deity that he will be deputed to judge the Irish on the day of doom. The forcefulness of the real Patrick's nature is coarsened by degrees into caricature, until he becomes the dictator who coerces an angel into making a bargain with him on the Mount of Murrisk. The image presented to the reader in the popular *Lives* of the bishop forms him as a hero saint.

The accounts of his acts were not written out of a historical interest, but simply for edification. And the monks, who dramatized both actual and legendary incidents, were not concerned with what manner of man he really was, but were guided instead by their knowledge of what popular taste demanded. The medieval hagiographer may be compared to the modern novelist; he provided literary recreation for the public, and had to consider the public taste. Patrick's life was adapted to an Irish ideal, and the earliest literature relating to his life seems to have been written in Irish. This literature must have been current in the sixth century, and on it the earliest Latin records are largely based.

But even as the writings of Patrick don't enable us to delineate his character, they do reveal an unmistakably strong personality and a spiritual nature. The man who wrote the *Confession* and the *Letter Against Coroticus* had strength of will, energy of action, resolution without over-confidence, and the capacity for resisting pressure from others. We also may infer that he was affectionate and sensitive, and a subtle analysis might disclose other traits. Perhaps most important, he possessed practical qualities that were essential for carrying through the task that he had been divinely inspired to fulfill. A rueful consciousness of the deficiencies of his education weighed on him throughout his career. We can feel this in his wearisome insistence upon his *rusticitas*. Also, he hasn't exaggerated his lack of culture; he writes in the style of a largely uneducated man. His Latin is as "rustic" as the Greek of St. Mark and St. Matthew.

From Patrick's Confession . . .

"Although I am imperfect in many things, I wish my brothers and acquaintances to know my dispositions, that they may be able to understand the desire of my soul. . . . Therefore, although I thought of writing long ago, I feared the censure of men, because I had not learned as the others who studied the sacred writings in the best way, and have never changed their language since their childhood, but continually learned it more perfectly, while I have to translate my words and speech into a foreign tongue. It can be easily proven from the style of my writings how I am instructed in speech and learning, for the Wise Man says: 'By the tongue wisdom Is discerned, and understanding and knowledge and learning by the word of the wise.' . . . I, in my old age, strive after that which I was hindered from learning in my youth. But who will believe me?"

187

Patrick was a *homo unius libri*, or "man with one book." But with that book, the Christian scriptures, he was extraordinarily familiar. His writings are crowded with scriptural sentences and phrases, most of them surely quoted from memory.

A Few Paragraphs Later . . .

"Therefore I undertook this work at first, though a rustic and a fugitive, and not knowing how to provide for the future. But this I know for certain: Before I was humbled, I was like a stone lying in deep mud, until He who is powerful came and in His mercy raised me up, and cared for me and placed me in His protection. Therefore I ought to cry out loudly, and thank the Lord for all his benefits, here and after, which the mind of man cannot estimate. Be amazed, both great and small who fear God; both rhetoricians and you of the Lord, hear who aroused me, a fool, from the midst of those who seem to be wise, and skilled in the law, and powerful in speech and in all things, inspiring me (if indeed I am) beyond others, even though I am despised by this world, so that, with fear and reverence and without murmuring, I will serve this nation faithfully, to whom the charity of Christ has transferred me, and given me for my life, if I shall survive. At last, with humility and truth, I will serve them."

Quoting the Bible

"There are . . . 72 books in the Bible; Patrick, in his few short pages makes reference or alludes to 54 of them. He also refers to twenty of those early Christian scholars, theologians and saints whom we know collectively as the Fathers of the Church; and finally, he makes reference to eight church councils. In other words, he is familiar with almost every major meeting of bishops and scholars down to his own time" (O Riordain, 16).

CHAPTER SEVENTEEN

Death and Burial

There are competing dates for the death of Patrick in the old sources, and AD 493 is chief among them. This is closely connected with the legendary theory that Patrick reached the age of 120. In one of the sources, it is stated that Patrick, having been captured in his twentieth year, was a slave for 15 years, studied for 40, and taught for 61. Hence it is inferred that he died at 111. There must be errors in those figures. In another source, we have the following statement: "baptized in seventh year, captured in tenth, was a slave for 7 years, studied for 30 years, and taught for 72." Hence his age at his death is inferred as 120 (10 + 7 + 30 + 72 = 119), the same as Moses. The Mosaic age, 120, wasn't handed down as a legend, and the true age

---

The Conclusion of Patrick's Confession . . .

"There is a sun we see that rises for us each day, but it will not rule or continue its splendor for ever, and all who adore it alone shall suffer miserably. But we who believe in and adore the true sun, Christ, who will never perish, and do His will, know that Christ will abide forever, reigning with God the Father Almighty and with the Holy Spirit, before the ages, and now, and for ever and ever. Amen. . . . I beg those who believe in and fear God, whoever may condescend to look into or receive this writing, which Patrick, the ignorant sinner, has written in Ireland, that no one may ever say, if I have ever done or demonstrated anything, however little. . . . But you judge, and let it be believed firmly, that it was the gift of God. And this is my confession before I die."

of some few years beyond 70 was not audaciously raised to the Mosaic figure for the purpose of the Mosaic comparison. The figure 120, or something approximate to it, was reached by means of a mistaken computation of chronological items.

His death is surrounded by legends that reflect the rival interests of Armagh, Downpatrick, and Saul, but attest to the fact that he died and was buried at the barn of Dichu. The people of Armagh were disappointed not to receive the saint's body, and it became ingenious as to how they explained these happenings. As the story goes, when the day of death drew near, an angel came and warned Patrick. Immediately afterwards, Patrick began to make preparations, and started for Armagh, which he loved above all other places. But as he went, a thorn bush burst into flames on the wayside and was not consumed. An angel spoke to Patrick, telling him to return to Saul. The angel granted him four petitions, as a consolation for the disappointment. Of the four, according to tradition, two of the petitions are significant. One was that the jurisdiction of his church would remain in Armagh. The other that the posterity of Dichu would never die out. The first represents the interests of Armagh, and the second clearly originated in Saul.

Patrick obeyed the command of the angel, who also predicted that his death would "set a boundary against night." The rite of the Eucharist was soon administered to him at Saul by Bishop Tassach of Raholp, and on March 17 he died and was buried at Saul.

After his death there was no night for twelve days, and people said that for a whole year the nights were less dark than usual. Other wonders were recorded, as well. People told how angels kept watch over his body and diffused, as they traveled back to heaven, sweet odors as of wine and honey.

But miracles of this kind weren't the only legends that gathered around the passing of the saint whom Armagh and Ulidia were both eager to appropriate. The old strife between the kingdom of Ulidia and the kingdom of Orior blazed up fresh, in story, over Patrick's grave. The men of Orior advanced into the island-plain of Saul, and blood would have been shed on the southern banks of Strangford Lough if a divine interposition hadn't stirred the waves of the bay into a sudden inundation that dispersed the hosts and

prevented a battle. Such inundations are actually a recurring motif in the legends of this part of Ireland.

All of this happened before the burial. But after the coveted body had been entombed, the men of Orior came again, resolved to snatch it from the grave. Finding a wagon drawn by oxen, they imagined the body was inside, and drove off, only to discover, when they were near Armagh, that no body was there. They had been the victims of an illusion, designed like the rising of the waters, to prevent the shedding of blood.

From these myths we can draw a negative inference: it is plain that, whatever controversy may have risen concerning the burial of Patrick, there was no armed conflict. The common motive of both legends is to account for the circumstance that the event didn't lead to a war between the two peoples. The story of the angel's appearance reflects a conciliation between the claims of Saul and the claims of Armagh, and the two legends of the frustrated attempts of the men of Orior embody the same motive of peace and concord. Armagh had to acquiesce in the fact that Saul possessed Patrick's body, and Saul acquiesced in the assertion that it was Patrick's own wish to lie in Armagh.

All of these tales took shape many years after Patrick's death. If his burial had actually caused any such commotion as the legends suppose, his tomb would have been conspicuous or well known. If these things had really taken place, there would have been no doubt as to the place where his body was laid. There would have been no room for conflicting claims. But so great was the uncertainty that it suggested a resemblance with Moses, whose grave was unknown. It is similarly recorded that St. Columba investigated and discovered the place of Patrick's sepulcher at Saul. All of these doubts and uncertainties justify us in concluding that Patrick was buried quietly in an unmarked grave, and that the pious excitement about his bones arose long after his death. We can feel little hesitation in deciding that the obscure grave was at Saul. Of the other places that come into the story, Saul alone needs no mythical support for its claim.

There are no visible memorials of Patrick, with one possible exception. In the Middle Ages, the church of Armagh cherished with superstitious veneration two treasures that were believed to have belonged to him: a pastoral staff and a handbell. The crosier was known as *baculus Jesu*, or the "Staff of Jesus," and we have records of its existence in Armagh as early as the eleventh century. It was transferred in the latter half of the twelfth century to the Cathedral of Christ Church of Dublin, and remained there for three centuries. In 1538, it was publicly burnt in High Street as an object of superstition by the first Protestant archbishop of Ireland, during the war of sixteenth-century zealots.

However, the quadrilateral iron handbell still exists. It is a four-sided bell, weighing three pounds, eight ounces, and made "of two plates of sheet-iron, which are bent over so as to meet, and are fastened by large-headed iron rivets." The handle is made of iron. The bell can be seen in the National Museum of Ireland in Dublin, where a shrine was built for it in about AD 1100. Both of these relics are ancient, and the black bell certainly existed at Armagh a hundred years or so after Patrick's death, but to say that it was his would be to go beyond our evidence.

St. Brigid of Ireland

The fascinating St. Brigid lived a century after Patrick, and there are many parallels between their lives. Both were raised in Christian homes; both began their religious careers in Leinster—Patrick by following in Palladius's path and Brigid by establishing her first convent in County Kildare on land given to her by the king of Leinster. Each of them battled the pagan traditions of the Druids, and often preserved remnants of pagan tradition in the midst of the new Christian religion. Brigid died in the early 520s, and tradition has her buried in Downpatrick, one of the towns that claims to be the burial place of St. Patrick (Downpatrick and Saul are within two miles of each other in County Down, in what is now Northern Ireland.) Her famous shoe, which is now called "The Shrine of St. Brigid's Shoe," can be found in the National Museum in Dublin.

Driving the Snakes Out of Ireland

Bury curiously avoids telling too much of the tale of that magical crosier. Perhaps he was wanting to avoid a discussion of the legend of Patrick driving the snakes out of Ireland, since those stories all return to the myth of this stick. Various legends exist as to how, where, and when Patrick was supposed to have obtained the staff. One such legend intimates that Jesus Christ himself had once used it—hence the name, *baculus Jesu*. Medieval Irish believers latched onto Patrick's comments in the *Confession* about being divinely instructed in his mission, as evidence that the crosier had been mystically passed from Jesus to Patrick, over a circuitous route spanning four centuries. Patrick is supposed to have used that staff to beat the snakes, symbolizing heathenism and evil, out of Ireland. Other legends tell it that the black bell mentioned by Bury was the tool for driving the snakes away. Legend has it that Patrick rang a bell from the summit of Croagh Patrick and then threw it over the side. Angels quickly retrieved the bell and returned it to him. Again and again this happened, and each time snakes and other crawling creatures fled. Interestingly, there still are no snakes in all of Ireland.

The Seventh-Century Biography by Muirchu

The Author, and the Book's Composition

The first formal biography that we possess, perhaps the first formal biography ever written, was composed by Muirchu towards the end of the seventh century. Muirchu is designated as *maccu Machtheni*, son or descendant of Machthene. But Muirchu himself refers to his father as Coguitosus, so there is room to wonder whether a natural or spiritual father is intended. We know, however, that Coguitosus had written some sort of a *Life* of St. Brigid of Kildare.

Muirchu lived in North Laigin, and perhaps he was specially associated with County Wicklow. He had a close association with Bishop Aed of Slebte, to whom he dedicated his book and from whom he derived material for it. The fact that he lived and wrote in the latter half of the seventh century is established by the date of the bishop's death, which is recorded in the annals as AD 700. Since Muirchu's book is dedicated to Aed, as still living, 699 is the lower limit for its composition. Or perhaps only for the composition of book I. Muirchu divided his work into two books. At the end of table of contents to book I, there occurs a notice that Aed helped him; perhaps book I was composed before, and book II, after, Aed's death.

The dedicatory preface to Bishop Aed is written in the most turgid style, and partly modeled on the opening verses of St. Luke's Gospel. Muirchu seems to declare that he is venturing upon a novel experiment, which had been tried before in Ireland only by his father (on Brigid). Muirchu aspired to do for Patrick what his father had done for Brigid. But in venturing into what he calls the "deep and perilous sea of sacred story," he may have been helped by Aed.

He used written sources. He refers to them in his preface, implying that the documents were anonymous. There is a marked contrast between the early portion of the biography up to Patrick's arrival in Ireland and the rest of the book. The early portion is free from the mythical element, but the narrative of Patrick's work in Ireland is characterized by its legendary setting. But even in this second part, Muirchu used written sources. A legendary narrative had been shaped and written down before his time. Thus, before the seventh century, the hagiographical literature that entertained the pious in Ireland was composed in their own language. It was not until the age of Cogitosus and Muirchu that a new departure was made, and people began to write Latin books on Irish saints.

Muirchu's Perspective

Muirchu belonged to that part of Ireland that had conformed to Roman religious practices since about AD 634. He probably took part in the Synod of Whitby in 664 that brought about the conformity of the north. It may be asked whether the *Life* of Patrick that Muirchu wrote at the wish of Aed had any intended purpose beyond its mere hagiographical interest. There is, I think, some reason for supposing that he had a particular motive. When Muirchu wrote, the church of Slebte had just been brought into close connection with Armagh. One medieval record relates, "Bishop Aed was in Slebte. He went to Armagh. He brought a bequest to Segene of Armagh, Segene gave another bequest to Aed, and Aed offered a bequest and his kin and his church to Patrick forever." It would be natural to bring this visit of Aed to Armagh, and his dedication of Slebte to Patrick, into connection with Muirchu's book.

Aed stimulated Muirchu to undertake the biography, and at that time, many people must have been trying to prepare the way for bringing about uniformity between northern and southern Ireland. The primary way of doing this was by inducing the north to accept the Roman religious practices which had, more than a generation earlier, been accepted by the south. It is reasonable to conjecture that Aed, who took part in the synod that brought about this result, was working toward it in his dealings with Armagh. And it certainly is possible that, in

How Patrick Is Portrayed in Art

"As a rule, St. Patrick is represented holding his Bishop's crosier, round about the staff of which a serpent is twined, in memory of the tradition that he drove all venomous snakes out of Ireland. Occasionally he is actually surrounded by serpents, who are shrinking away from him in terror, and now and then a harp, one of the national emblems of Ireland, replaces the crosier, some say because of the fervor of the saint's intercession for his adopted country after his death. . . . Now and then St. Patrick is represented kneeling at the feet of Pope Celestine, from whom he is receiving his decretals as missionary Bishop of Ireland, but a more favorite subject is the Baptism of a certain King, whose foot the Bishop is said to have wounded by accidentally dropping the point of his crosier upon it. The neophyte took no notice of the wound, thinking its infliction was part of the Christian ceremony, and St. Patrick did not observe it, until he saw a stream of blood staining the ground" (Bell, 246–247).

giving such a prominent place in his narrative to the legend of Patrick's first Easter in Ireland, Muirchu was thinking of that synodical Easter controversy.

It is significant that just on the eve of the reconciliation of north and south, an ecclesiastic of southern Ireland whose name is associated with that reconciliation, should have given to the world a *Life* of Patrick. If the book had come down to us anonymously, we would have probably imagined it to have been written in the north, and we would perhaps have guessed that it came from Armagh.

Muirchu's *Life* had a marked influence on all subsequent biographies of Ireland's saint. It established a framework of narrative that later compilers adopted, fitting in material from other sources.

SOURCES

Ashe, Geoffrey, ed. *The Quest for Arthur's Britain*. St. Albans, UK: Granada Publishing, 1971.

The Venerable Bede. *The Ecclesiastical History of England*. Christian Classics Ethereal Library: http://www.ccel.org/ccel/bede/history.toc.html.

Bell, Mrs. Arthur. *Lives and Legends of the Great Hermits and Fathers of the Church, with other Contemporary Saints*. London: George Bell & Sons, 1902.

Binchy, D.A. "Patrick and His Biographers." *Studia Hibernica* 2 (1962).

Bitel, Lisa M. "Saints and Angry Neighbors: The Politics of Cursing in Irish Hagiography." In *Monks & Nuns, Saints & Outcasts: Religion in Medieval Society*, edited by Sharon Farmer and Barbara H. Rosenwein. Ithaca, NY: Cornell University Press, 2000.

Bryce, James. *The Holy Roman Empire*. London: Macmillan and Company, 1904.

Bury, J.B. *A History of Freedom of Thought*. New York: Henry Holt, 1913.

Casson, Lionel. *The Ancient Mariners: Seafarers and Sea Fighters of the Mediterranean in Ancient Times*. London: Victor Gollancz Ltd., 1959.

Croinin, Daibhi O., ed. *A New History of Ireland*. Vol. 1, *Prehistoric and Early Ireland*. New York: Oxford University Press, 2005.

Duffy, Eamon. *Saints & Sinners: A History of the Popes*. 2nd ed. New Haven: Yale University Press, 2001.

Farmer, D.H., ed. *The Age of Bede*. Translated by J.F. Webb. New York: Penguin Books, 1983.

Fedotov, George P. *The Russian Religious Mind: Kievan Christianity*. Cambridge: Harvard University Press, 1946.

Freeman, Philip. *St. Patrick of Ireland: A Biography*. New York: Simon and Schuster, 2004.

Hanson, R.P.C. *St. Patrick: His Origins and Career*. New York: Oxford University Press, 1968.

Herren, Michael W., and Shirley Ann Brown. *Christ in Celtic Christianity: Britain and Ireland from the Fifth to the Tenth Century*. Rochester, NY: The Boydell Press, 2002.

Hood, A.B.E. *St. Patrick: His Writings and Muirchu's Life*. Chichester: Phillimore and Co., 1978.

Kavanagh, Patrick. *Tarry Flynn*. New York: Penguin Books, 1980.

Moran, Patrick Francis. *Essays on the Origin, Doctrines and Discipline of the Early Irish Church*. Dublin: James Duffy, 1864.

O Riordain, John J. *Early Irish Saints*. Dublin: The Columba Press, 2001.

Rhys, John. *Celtic Britain*. London: S.P.C.K., 1882.

Russo, Daniel G. *Town Origins and Development in Early England, c. 400–950 A.D.* Westport, CT: Greenwood Press, 1998.

Ryan, John, SJ. *Irish Monasticism: Origins and Early Development.* Dublin: The Talbot Press, 1931.

Thomas, Charles. *Christianity in Roman Britain to A.D. 500.* Berkeley: University of California Press, 1981.

Thompson, E.A. *Who Was Saint Patrick?* New York: St. Martin's Press, 1985.

Zimmer, Heinrich. *The Celtic Church in Britain and Ireland.* Translated by A. Meyer. London: David Nutt, 1902.

ACKNOWLEDGMENTS

Many thanks to Professor Steven Swayne for his help in obtaining source materials. Thanks, too, to the Dartmouth College libraries. The two maps reproduced in this book are taken from the original edition of Bury's biography of St. Patrick. The wall mosaic pictured on the frontispiece hangs in Westminster Cathedral, London, and the photograph of it was taken by the editor.

INDEX

ABOUT PARACLETE PRESS

Who We Are

Paraclete Press is a publisher of books, recordings, and DVDs on Christian spirituality. Our publishing represents a full expression of Christian belief and practice—from Catholic to Evangelical, from Protestant to Orthodox.

We are the publishing arm of the Community of Jesus, an ecumenical monastic community in the Benedictine tradition. As such, we are uniquely positioned in the marketplace without connection to a large corporation and with informal relationships to many branches and denominations of faith.

What We Are Doing

Books • Paraclete publishes books that show the richness and depth of what it means to be Christian. Although Benedictine spirituality is at the heart of all that we do, we publish books that reflect the Christian experience across many cultures, time periods, and houses of worship. We publish books that nourish the vibrant life of the church and its people—books about spiritual practice, formation, history, ideas, and customs.

We have several different series, including the best-selling Paraclete Essentials and Paraclete Giants series of classic texts in contemporary English; A Voice from the Monastery—men and women monastics writing about living a spiritual life today; award-winning poetry; best-selling gift books for children on the occasions of baptism and first communion; and the Active Prayer Series that brings creativity and liveliness to any life of prayer.

Recordings • From Gregorian chant to contemporary American choral works, our music recordings celebrate sacred choral music through the centuries. Paraclete distributes the recordings of the internationally acclaimed choir Gloriæ Dei Cantores, praised for their "rapt and fathomless spiritual intensity" by *American Record Guide*, and the Gloriæ Dei Cantores Schola, which specializes in the study and performance of Gregorian chant. Paraclete is also the exclusive North American distributor of the recordings of the Monastic Choir of St. Peter's Abbey in Solesmes, France, long considered to be a leading authority on Gregorian chant.

Videos • Our videos offer spiritual help, healing, and biblical guidance for life issues: grief and loss, marriage, forgiveness, anger management, facing death, and spiritual formation.

Learn more about us at our website:
www.paracletepress.com, or call us toll-free at 1-800-451-5006.

SCAN
TO
READ
MORE

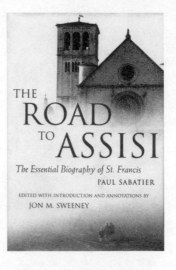